The Early Years Curriculum

The Early Years Curriculum

Edited by:

Lynn Ang
Senior Lecturer, Institute of Education, University of London

With contributions from:

Carolyn Silberfeld
Senior Lecturer, Cass School of Education and Communities,
University of East London

Karen Horsley
Lecturer, Cass School of Education and Communities,
University of East London

Ruksana Mohammed
Lecturer, Cass School of Education and Communities,
University of East London

Prithvi Perepa
Senior Lecturer, Cass School of Education and Communities,
University of East London

John Trushell
Principal Lecturer, Cass School of Education and Communities,
University of East London

Jane Cox
Senior Lecturer, Cass School of Education and Communities,
University of East London

Routledge
Taylor & Francis Group

LONDON AND NEW YORK

First published 2014
by Routledge
2 Park Square, Milton Park, Abingdon, Oxon OX14 4RN

and by Routledge
711 Third Avenue, New York, NY 10017

Routledge is an imprint of the Taylor & Francis Group, an informa business

British Library Cataloguing in Publication Data
A catalogue record for this book is available from the British Library

Library of Congress Cataloging in Publication Data
A catalog record for this book is available from the Library of Congress

ISBN: 978-0-415-73582-7 (hbk)
ISBN: 978-1-408-22332-1 (pbk)
ISBN: 978-1-315-81521-3 (ebk)

Typeset in 11.25/14pt Minion by 75

Printed and bound in Great Britain by
TJ International Ltd, Padstow, Cornwall

Contents

Contributors

Dr Lynn Ang is Senior Lecturer in Early Childhood at the Institute of Education (IoE), University of London. From 2003 to 2012 she was based at the Cass School of Education and Communities at the University of East London, where she was Programme Leader for the MA in Early Childhood Studies and a supervisor of Doctorate students. Her research specialisms include the early years curriculum, leadership and the early years workforce, and early childhood across cultures. She has worked in Singapore, Scotland and now England. She has published in various international journals and holds a number of research grant awards. She is a Fellow of the ESRC Peer Review College. Her publications include 'Leading and managing in the early years: a study of the impact of a NCSL programme on children's centre leaders' perceptions of leadership and practice' in the *Journal of Educational Management, Administration and Leadership (EMAL)* (2012), 40(3), pp. 289–304 and *Early Childhood Education in a Diverse Society: An ethnographic study of preschools in Singapore* (2011), Singapore: Singapore Committee of OMEP (World Organisation for Early Childhood Education), ISBN 978-981-08-9373-6.

Carolyn Silberfeld has been actively involved in developing and leading early childhood studies undergraduate programmes for 19 years, the past 12 years of which have been at the University of East London. She has a background in children's nursing, midwifery and health visiting, practising until 1991 both in the UK and Burkina Faso, West Africa. Between 1991 and 1993 Carolyn developed and led the post registration research programme and developed the Diploma in Community Health at Thames Valley University. She is one of the founding members of the Early Childhood Studies Degrees Network and has participated in all the working groups relating to practice and benchmark statements. Carolyn has a particular interest in international student exchange programmes and reflective learning, and her recent research focuses on the longer term impact on students' personal, academic and professional/practice development following a period of study abroad. She has strong links with early years education and training in several local authorities and continues to lead the modules relating to fieldwork and practice in early years settings.

Karen Horsley is a lecturer in Early Childhood Studies at the University of East London, having completed the degree herself, with first class honours in 2004. She has worked with young children, families and professionals in a variety of settings and contexts including women's refuge, child development centre, and local nurseries and primary schools. Karen completed her Post Graduate Certificate in Learning and Teaching in Higher Education and is a Fellow of The Higher Education Academy. She has recently qualified as an Early Years Professional. Karen's research interests include the development of language and literacy in young children and her current research interest focuses on the ways in which professional and practitioners recognise and respond to the diversity of children's developmental needs.

Ruksana Mohammed is an experienced early childhood practitioner and manager who has worked across many early years provisions, and has worked with the continually changing curriculum since 1996 within her practice. She is currently Programme Leader for the Early Years Professional Status at the Cass School of Education and Communities in the University of East London. She maintains a keen involvement with early years settings and early childhood practitioners.

Prithvi Perepa is a senior lecturer at the University of East London and teaches on the undergraduate and postgraduate special education programmes at the University. He started his career as a teacher for children on the autism spectrum. He has many years of experience of working with children with autism and their families. He has worked in various roles in the field of autism including being an Advisory teacher for Early Years and Development Officer for the National Autistic Society's Black and Minority Ethnic Communities Project. One of his research interests is culture and autism, which has also been the subject of his doctoral research.

John Trushell lectures on Linguistics in Education and is programme leader of the MA in English Language Teaching at the University of East London. He has conducted research into language, literacy and ICT — word processing, interactive books, adventure games etc — since 1983. His publications include a special issue of the *Journal of Research in Reading* concerning computers and literacy which he co-edited.

Jane Cox is a Senior Lecturer of Early Childhood Studies at the University of East London. She has taught on a range of undergraduate and postgraduate modules, particularly those relating to policy and research. She has also supervised

MA students. Her research interests centre on how children are portrayed in the news media and the condition of contemporary childhood. She has a first degree in Early Childhood Studies and Social Science. Jane was awarded a PhD (Education) in 2005; her thesis is titled 'Childhood in crisis: myth, reality or cause for concern? Perspectives from children, parents and the news media.' She has a Postgraduate Certificate in Learning and Teaching in Higher Education and is a Fellow of the Higher Education Academy.

Acknowledgements

My heartfelt thanks to all the contributors for their commitment and patience throughout the writing process. Thank you for believing in the value of this book and writing this journey with me.

The contributors and I would like to thank all colleagues in the Cass School of Education and Communities at the University of East London who supported and shared their interest in this project along the way.

Our grateful thanks also to the many practitioners, children and students for providing the inspiration which brought this book to life.

1

Introduction

The curriculum in diverse settings: defining curriculum

Lynn Ang

Contextualising the curriculum

With early childhood education and care (ECEC) increasingly high on the global agenda with many governments, the early childhood curriculum is firmly placed within an international setting. The impetus for this book is to explore the purpose, function and influence of the curriculum on children's learning and development across a range of settings. The purpose of this book is to understand the values, philosophies, theories and ideologies that underpin different approaches to the curriculum – in other words, our understanding and assumptions about how and what young children learn within their care and educational environment. For every early childhood professional, a perennial concern about their practice revolves around two key questions: what should children learn (the content of the curriculum) and how best do they learn (the pedagogy and learning that underpin the curriculum)? These questions provide a starting point from which to explore the values and knowledge that inform the way the curriculum is shaped. More importantly, they provide a basis for educators to reflect critically on the source and currency of their own knowledge and pedagogy, as they develop their understanding of early childhood education and care. These questions are particularly important, not least because of the rapid changes in government policy in a fast-developing sector such as that in the United Kingdom, as well as the proliferation of research in the early childhood field.

In the global report *Start Strong II: Early childhood education and care* by the Organisation for Economic Co-operation and Development (OECD), the provision of quality early childhood education and care was recognised as an essential and high-priority area. The report states that '[t]he provision of quality early childhood education and care (ECEC) has remained firmly on government agendas in recent years. Public awareness of gaps in provision and of insufficient quality in services has moved the issue of child care and after-school care onto electoral agendas in many countries' (OECD, 2006). The report provides an account of the issues and debates that take place in the early childhood sector in twelve countries around the world, and the developments that occur within specific countries across Europe and the United Kingdom in their drive to transform the early years sector and improve services for children.

With specific reference to the early years curriculum, the OECD also published a report in 2004 by its Directorate of Education entitled *Starting Strong: Curricula and pedagogies in early childhood education and care. Five curriculum outlines* (OECD, 2004). The report marked the culmination of a cross-country project launched in 1998 on the 'Thematic Review of Early Childhood Education and Care Policy', aimed at improving access to and quality of early childhood education and care. As part of an extensive review of early childhood policies globally, the report on curricula and pedagogies explored the knowledge base and research of early childhood programmes across five countries: the experiential education approach in Flanders and the Netherlands; the High/Scope Curriculum in the United States; the Reggio Emilia Approach in Italy; *Te Whāriki* in New Zealand; and the Swedish curriculum. While the report provides useful insights into each curricula model, it also raises pertinent issues with regards to the quality and diversity of early childhood curricula. It contends that while countries approach and define curricula in different ways, there is an overarching need to ensure that the quality and impact of early childhood curricula are sustained at the highest possible standard of practice and delivery. Significantly, the report emphasises the importance of taking into account the knowledge base and values that underpin our different approaches to the curriculum, the thinking and learning processes that work best for young children, and the implications of this for early years professionals and their practice. These findings from the international community have heightened debates around issues relating to the curriculum, pedagogy and the way countries govern early childhood services in general.

In England, the issues foregrounded in the OECD reports help to contextualise the major policy drivers undertaken in recent years to raise the quality of early years provision in terms of accessibility, equality, curriculum and pedagogy (OECD, 2006). The early years sector has continued to evolve in a dynamic sea of change, in particular with regards to policy developments. The review of the

Early Years Foundation Stage (EYFS) established in the Tickell report (Tickell, 2011) precipitated the introduction of a revised statutory curriculum, with key recommendations to reduce the number of early learning goals and place fewer bureaucratic demands on practitioners to fulfil statutory assessment requirements when delivering the curriculum (DfE, 2012). Following the introduction of the revised EYFS, an independent review of early years professional qualifications was undertaken and published in the final report, *Foundations for Quality. The independent review of early education and childcare qualifications* (Nutbrown, 2012). The report provided a timely review of the early years workforce, with proposals to improve the professionalism of the workforce by raising the standards of professional training and qualifications. One of the recommendations from the report, for instance, is to move towards a minimum level of qualification for early years practitioners: 'Ultimately, the long term target should be that all staff counting against the staff:child ratios in the EYFS should possess at least a "full and relevant" level 3 qualification' (Nutbrown, 2012). These reforms continue to shape the shifting landscape of the early years sector, with implications for the role of early years professionals in delivering and shaping the curriculum.

Defining curriculum

The very notion of curriculum is elusive as its meaning is often open to multiple interpretations. The concept of 'curriculum' gives rise to many different perspectives and theories, and these vary not only according to those who deliver it but among those who learn from it. These interpretations of 'curriculum' are crucial as they in turn serve as sources of curriculum decisions made at the level of policy and practice. It is therefore immensely important that we investigate various approaches to and definitions of curriculum to help us identify the philosophical and epistemological roots that shape much of current thinking about young children's learning and development.

Early definitions of curriculum tended to espouse an aspirational model of education by which children are taught and towards which they are guided. Spodek (1973), for example, argues that curriculum models are idealised descriptions of programmes that can be copied or emulated. Evans (1982) states that 'a curriculum model provides an ideal representation of the essential philosophical, administrative, and pedagogical components of a grand education plan'. Both definitions suggest a somewhat 'ideal' model of education and the role of educators in the pursuit of achieving such a vision. In another early definition, Tanner and Tanner (1980) define the curriculum as a highly prescriptive learning experience, which follows a formulaic construction of knowledge and experiences that contributes to the accumulative growth of the individual's competence. As they write, the curriculum is:

> the planned and guided learning experiences and intended outcomes, formulated through the systematic reconstruction of knowledge and experiences under the auspices of the school, for the learners' continuous and wilful growing in personal and social competence.

However, as recent paradigms emerge, particularly about the sociology of childhood, this notion of curricula as an idealised and highly structured educational framework becomes untenable. The growing literature regarding sociocultural theory and the importance of situating children's learning and development within their sociocultural contexts and developing sociocultural beliefs has led to significant shifts in our understanding of the curriculum. In the journal paper 'New directions: charting the paths for the role of sociocultural theory in early childhood education and curriculum', Edwards (2003) argues for the importance of sociocultural values and their influence on the way the curriculum is shaped:

> The creation of curriculum is a human endeavour, and like all human endeavours involves the cultural values, beliefs, assumptions, theories and languages of its developers in its very construction. Defining curriculum therefore becomes a task of identifying not only course content, but also the particular cultural values and theoretical constructs on which it has been based.

From a sociocultural perspective, the curriculum is therefore embedded within its particular social, cultural and historical context, and is a product of its time and culture. Decisions about the content of the curriculum and how it is delivered are informed by society's understanding and assumptions of how children develop and learn, and determined by its purpose and function (what and who the curriculum is for). As a cultural and social construct, the early childhood curriculum is therefore an educational framework which reflects larger societal concerns and expectations. They help shape government and public expectations of what and how children should learn, even though these can at times be different from those held by early childhood practitioners. As the 2004 OECD report explicitly states, we are all embedded in culture and the curriculum can never be copied from somewhere else but 'must be developed in the historical and cultural context of each country'. The report lays an important claim in broadening our current understanding of the concept of curriculum. By adopting a sociocultural approach, it acknowledges the complexity of the way curriculum models develop, and the reality that there are no two curricula that are exactly the same and there therefore cannot be any replication.

The construction of the early childhood curriculum has immense implications for early years professionals. As a framework of practice, the curriculum provides an educational structure and direction for educators in their work to support and develop the competencies and skills of young children (Sylva *et al.*, 1999). The curriculum provides a conceptual framework for educators' decision making in terms of planning and setting their educational priorities, policies and teaching practices. The body of knowledge that influences the way the curriculum is shaped is therefore crucial, as it gives us a clue as to how the curriculum is determined and by whom. Historically, during the 1980s and 1990s, theories of child development were the dominant theoretical foundation for constructing the curriculum (Silin, 1987; Spodek, 1986; Spodek and Saracho, 1991; Weber, 1984). This meant that how learning took place and what was taught in settings were determined by psychological concepts of how children developed. This theory was influenced predominantly by the work of the developmental psychologist Jean Piaget. According to Piagetian theory, children develop in a linear, predictable progression along identifiable milestones or stages, but the environment in which their development takes place is somewhat de-emphasised and irrelevant. A major criticism of this paradigm was the cultural appropriateness of using developmental theory as an underpinning paradigm for learning, and the universal application of the curriculum for children whose cultural and social backgrounds can be very diverse, and whose development does not always conform to a hierarchical, organised sequence.

As research in early childhood education advanced, the work of Vygotsky (1978) and later Rogoff (1984, 1998) presented an alternative paradigm for the curriculum, emphasising the importance of the social context and collaborative process of learning. As a cultural psychologist, Vygotsky, unlike Piaget, stressed the social nature of development and how learning is context dependent. At the core of Vygotsky's work is the notion that children develop best as a result of their interactions with the sociocultural environment and the world around them. Building on Vygotsky's theory, Rogoff went on to argue that children developed cognitively through participation in their sociocultural contexts, either by observing or participating actively in their interactions within the community and society. Children would then develop their own cultural norms or cultural competence in order to interact effectively with those around them. The work of Bronfenbrenner (1979), an American psychologist, has also made significant contributions to our understanding of how children develop in their sociocultural contexts and of the interactions that take place within them.

Bronfenbrenner's ecological model consists of a series of 'nested' structures which signify the complex layers of influence on children's development. Referred to as the microsystem, mesosystem, exosystem and macrosystem, each of these integrated layers demonstrates the inter-relationships between the child, family, community and society, and the powerful impact they have on children's development.

The ideas of cultural theorists such as Bronfenbrenner, Vygotsky and Rogoff offer a more differentiated understanding of the contextual influences on children's development by recognising the extent to which children's development is mediated first and foremost through their wider social, cultural and political environments. This focus on the wider context of learning has informed much of current practice in early years settings today, where collaborative learning, play and interaction – encouraging cooperative relationships among children and between children and adults, and ensuring learning is situated within sociocultural contexts – have become central tenets. What seems to take precedence is the importance of taking into account a holistic perspective of children's development and creating an environment that is conducive to exploring, learning and constructing, and which is meaningful to the child. The relevance of sociocultural theory for contemporary understanding of the early childhood curriculum is therefore pervasive, especially in the way that it has shaped our knowledge of how children's learning can be developed and supported.

The influence of sociocultural theory is not only pertinent but also far reaching in the way that it informs cross-cultural research in the field, more specifically in the Asia-Pacific region, where early years curricula are often perceived as unique learning environments and distinct cultures for learning. In an ethnographic study of the early years curriculum in Singapore, Ang (2010) argues:

> Vygotsky's ideas inform us of the importance of adopting a holistic perspective of early childhood education. More importantly, it also emphasises the significance of taking into account a cross-cultural perspective, not least because children develop and learn in the context of their culture and society, and one is inconceivable without another.

Key questions

The chapters that follow will therefore seek to explore the different knowledge base and models of the early childhood curriculum. They will aim to understand the sociocultural dimensions of the teaching and learning experience, the purpose and role of the curriculum and its impact on children's development and learning. Throughout the discussions in this book, key questions arise:

- What does it mean to provide an effective early childhood curriculum?
- As practitioners and students of early childhood, how do we know if the setting is providing an appropriate curriculum and how do we know if it is effective or even appropriate for the children?
- How do educators maintain the quality of their curriculum and service? Is providing additional funding and resources the only solution?
- Who defines what is a quality curriculum? How can we define a quality curriculum when quality itself is such a dynamic and complex concept, influenced by values and beliefs, and closely bound up with culture and context?
- How can the curriculum address issues of inclusion and inequalities?
- How can we deliver the curriculum in a way that ensures all children, regardless of their background, are able to participate fully in a quality early years provision?

There are no easy answers to these questions, but what they provide are starting points for reflection and new challenges from which to explore the pertinent issues and debates that surround our understanding of the curriculum. What is clear is that all early childhood settings, regardless of their type or function, have a responsibility to deliver a curriculum that serves the needs and interests of the child, and one which develops children's learning. To do so would certainly mean that the child's cultural and social context must be taken into account in all its complexities.

To deliver an appropriate and quality curriculum also means evaluating its impact and effectiveness on the children and their learning. It is my fervent belief that a curriculum or experience of learning is only ever effective if it is meaningful to the child. To this end, the impact and effectiveness of the curriculum ought to be part of a continuous process of review and evaluation. The 2004 OECD curriculum report emphasises the importance of accountability in the early childhood field. It stresses the need to develop regular evaluations and assessments of early childhood programmes in the search for quality care and education: 'Curricula should be evaluated and validated, especially the effect of their programme on children's long-term learning and development' (OECD 2004). For early childhood professionals, this means constantly reviewing and evaluating their values and beliefs. It entails not only asking the questions 'What are we doing with the children?' and 'What sort of learning are we providing?', but also 'Why do we do it?' and 'How can we do it even better?'.

Early childhood professionals and all those involved in the care and education of young children must find room in their practice to explore, try things out and raise difficult questions even when there are no fixed or final answers. In the report *Foundations for Quality* (Nutbrown, 2012), the role of early years professionals is recognised as central to the UK government's drive to raise the quality of the workforce and improve services for young children. The report states: 'Practitioners are the most valuable asset in any early years setting. They are the single biggest contributor to the quality of provision, and they can be the driving force towards improvement.' The report makes clear that early years practitioners are expected to maintain the highest standards of professional practice and competency in their work with children. Their role in the setting is key to ensuring that an ethical and effective care and education environment is maintained to maximise children's learning and development. Within such an environment, and at the heart of any curriculum, must surely be the rights and interests of the child. It is only when educators are involved in an ongoing process of dialogue and reflection about their pedagogy and practice that they can begin the journey of conceiving a quality curriculum.

The chapters

The overarching aim of this book is to explore different ways of understanding the early years curriculum, while developing a critical awareness of how children and childhoods are viewed from a range of educational settings. Each of the following chapters is grounded in a specific curricular model, with a discussion of the curriculum's educational objectives, content and structure, underpinning philosophies, theoretical tensions and implications on practice. The different curriculum approaches will reflect the differences in the value commitments concerning what is less or more important for young children to learn as well as the intentions behind the curriculum. The discussions will also highlight how different interpretations of the same theoretical paradigm can generate distinctive approaches to the curriculum. Taken together, the chapters contend that young children learn in many different ways but that fundamental principles remain – that the learning, teaching and construction of a curriculum cannot be separated from the sociocultural context of the children and the society in which they live.

To this end, each chapter includes a list of questions to help readers reflect and critique the notion of a 'universal curriculum' and to recognise the many different models that exist in local and international contexts. Chapter 2, by Silberfeld and Horsley, explores the issues and debates that surround the revised Early

Years Foundation Stage (EYFS) (DfE, 2012) as a statutory curriculum for all preschool settings in England. The chapter offers a critical discussion of the factors that influence the curriculum, and the implications of the EYFS on professional practice and the early years workforce. Continuing the dialogue on the EYFS is Chapter 3 on 'The challenges of implementing an early years curriculum' by Mohammed, which offers a distinct but equally insightful discussion about the English curriculum, as seen through the eyes of an early years professional who is currently in practice. Both chapters set out the complex challenges and demands in delivering a curriculum which aims to serve the great diversity of children and families, all of whom are living in a culturally diverse and fast-changing community. The reflective questions at the end of each chapter provoke readers to delve deeper into their own understanding of the curriculum and what it means to be an 'early childhood professional' in England.

The next two chapters, by Weston and Perepa bring to the fore the important themes of inclusion and special education. Chapter 4 discusses the ways in which children's physical and intellectual development are closely interwoven during the early years, and how the curriculum can be an important medium in facilitating and supporting children's exploration and play. The discussion raises pertinent questions about adopting the appropriate pedagogical approaches and physical learning within a truly inclusive early years curriculum. Chapter 5 extends the debate on inclusion from a new perspective, with an in-depth discussion of culture, autism and the interactions between the two concepts. Perepa's premise that Autism Spectrum Disorder (ASD) is a developmental disability that impacts on individuals in three main aspects – social interaction, social communication and flexibility of thinking – provides invigorating ideas about how we define and indeed view children who are living with the condition. The chapter brings home the fact that in a multicultural society like Britain, different cultural groups hold different sets of norms, and this becomes especially problematic when conditions such as autism are being diagnosed on the basis of particular behaviour exhibited by individual children, often divorced from any cultural relevance.

Chapter 6 by Trushell provides an in-depth account of the interface between early literacy as a traditional visual and oral learning process and one that takes place in a technologically enhanced environment in the contemporary classroom. The discussion addresses pertinent issues such as the appropriateness of using information and communication technology (ICT) in enhancing children's literacy and the potential of using new technologies such as electronic storybooks to induce new pedagogies and approaches to learning. Looking beyond the English context, Chapter 7 on Reggio Emilia, by Cox, and Chapter 8 on the Singapore context, by Ang, provide alternative views of how the curriculum is constructed in two international contexts. The former discusses an innovative approach to early years education, and the distinctiveness of the Reggio approach in supporting children's development and learning. The chapter addresses the notion of transferability of curricula models, a pertinent issue that underpins the book as a whole as it discusses the implications of transplanting and commodifying one curriculum model to another context. Chapter 8 offers another interesting insight into a distinct approach to learning – the Singapore *A Framework for a Kindergarten Curriculum*. The chapter provides an original and unique perspective of how early learning and education is conceptualised in one country in Southeast Asia.

The book as a whole presents critical discussions of the early years curriculum and how different philosophical and theoretical paradigms on the knowledge of the child and childhood influence the way the curriculum is designed and delivered. Together, the chapters raise key questions about the knowledge base of early childhood theory, philosophy and practice: How do we know *what works* in early childhood? For whom does it work? And to what ends? The chapters are important in opening up new ideas and debates about the early years curriculum, and the professional knowledge that is required in guiding the thinking of early childhood students and professionals. Ultimately, the early childhood curriculum takes on many forms and is interpreted in many different ways. There is no universal agreement about what constitutes an effective early years curriculum. Each curriculum is set within a specific social and cultural context, and these have a strong influence on the way programmes and practices are implemented and shaped within early years settings.

References

Ang, L. (2010) 'Cross-cultural perspectives in early childhood education: Vygotskian influences and ethnographic insights into one preschool in East Asia, Singapore', in Tuna A. and Hayden J. (eds.) *Early Childhood Programs as the Doorway to Social Cohesion: Application of Vygotsky's ideas from an East–West perspective*, Newcastle upon Tyne: Cambridge Scholars Publishing.

Bronfenbrenner, U. (1979) *The Ecology of Human Development*, Cambridge, MA: Harvard University Press.

Department for Education (DfE) (2012) *Statutory Framework for the Early Years Foundation Stage: Setting the standards for learning, development and care for children from birth to five.* Available online at: www.education.gov.uk/publications/standard/AllPublications/Page1/DFE-00023-2012.

Edwards, S. (2003) 'New directions: charting the paths for the role of sociocultural theory in early childhood education and curriculum', *Contemporary Issues in Early Childhood*, 4(3), 251–66.

Evans, E. D. (1982) 'Curriculum models', in Spodek, B. (ed.) *Handbook of Research in Early Childhood Education*, New York: Free Press.

Nutbrown, C. (2012) *Foundations for Quality. The independent review of early education and childcare qualifications*, Cheshire: Department for Education. Available online at: www. education.gov.uk/publications/standard/publicationDetail/Page1/DFE-00068-2012

OECD (2004) *Starting Strong: Curricula and pedagogies in early childhood education and care. Five curriculum outlines*, Paris: OECD Publications.

OECD (2006) *Start Strong II: Early childhood education and care*, Paris: OECD Publications.

Rogoff, B. (1984) 'Introduction: thinking and learning in social context', in Rogoff, B. and Lave, J. (eds.) *Everyday Cognition: Its development in social context*, Cambridge, MA: Harvard University Press.

Rogoff, B. (1998) 'Cognition as a collaborative process', in Damon, W. (ed.) *Handbook of Child Psychology*, New York: John Wiley.

Silin, J. G. (1987) 'The early childhood educator's knowledge base: a reconsideration', in Katz, L. and Steiner, K. (eds.) *Current Topics in Early Childhood Education*, Norwood, NJ: Ablex.

Spodek, B. (1973) *Early Childhood Education*, Upper Saddle River, NJ: Prentice Hall.

Spodek, B. (1986) 'Development, values and knowledge in the kindergarten curriculum', in Spodek, B. (ed.) *Today's Kindergarten: Exploring the knowledge base. Expanding the curriculum*, New York: Teachers College Press.

Spodek, B. and Saracho, O. N. (1991) *Issues in Early Childhood Curriculum*, New York: Teachers College Press.

Sylva, K., Melhuish, E., Sammons, P. and Siraj-Blatchford, I. (1999) *The Effective Provision of Pre-school Education (EPPE) Project – A longitudinal study funded by the DfEE/ 1997–2003)*, University of London: Institute of Education.

Tanner, D. and Tanner, N. (1980) *Curriculum Development: Theory into practice* (2nd Edition), New York: Macmillan.

Tickell, C. (2011) *The Early Years: Foundations for life, health and learning, an Independent Report on the Early Years Foundation Stage to Her Majesty's Government*, Nottingham: DfE.

Vygotsky, L. (1978) *Mind in Society: The development of higher psychological processes*, Cambridge, MA: Harvard University Press.

Weber, E. (1984) *Ideas Influencing Early Childhood Education: A theoretical analysis*, New York: Teachers College Press.

2

The Early Years Foundation Stage curriculum in England: a missed opportunity?

Carolyn Helena Silberfeld and Karen Horsley

'There's no time to talk about fish fingers and "standy up" yoghurts because we are too busy doing literacy, maths and reading!' (Mia, aged 5)

Overview

This chapter explores the potential for alternative interpretations of the Early Years Foundation Stage (EYFS), which demonstrate how young children's learning and development can be encouraged, sustained and extended within the contexts of children's lived experiences. It will interrogate the context in which the EYFS was introduced as a statutory curriculum in 2008, having been driven by different demands and agendas of stakeholders, and will discuss the implications for early years professional practice in the new streamlined EYFS implemented in September 2012. It will explore alternative pathways to understanding and facilitating children's learning and development within early years settings, both nationally and internationally. This chapter will explore the value and purpose of the EYFS in terms of how it supports children's learning and development in early years settings. Missed opportunities can occur as practitioners strive to meet very different and complex demands placed on them by society, policy makers and regulatory bodies.

Key Themes

- Developments in the EYFS and the way in which children's learning and development can be encouraged.
- Different interpretations of the EYFS which can lead to missed opportunities.
- The complexity of decision making and meeting the recommendations of the EYFS.
- Cross-cultural examples of early years practice.

What did you do at nursery today?

'Well, first I sat at the dough table and rolled the dough in my hands. Lucy said hers was a snake and mine, mine was a worm. Mrs Pitt talked about long ones and short ones, fat ones and thin ones, and Mummy, Katie rolled her dough so long it went right over the end of the table. And nobody said, "What are you going to make? A cake would be nice."'

'Yes, but then what did you do?'

'I played on the climbing frame and, do you know Mummy, I climbed to the very top and had great fun sliding down, and Mrs Crompton gave me a clap and said, "Well done!"'

'Yes, but did you do anything today?'

'Megan and I went to the paint table. It was lovely and gooey and we made lots of patterns with our fingers and hands. Megan had yellow paint and I had red, and Mummy, Miss Howard said, "I wonder what would happen if your paint got mixed up?" and Mummy, do you know what, the paint went orange! And no one said, "What a mess you've made."'

'Yes, but what else have you done?'

'At milk time we sat in a circle and talked about our friends. Mummy, I told Mrs Crompton that my best friend is Luke because he came to see if I was alright when I fell and hurt my knee outside. And do you know, Mummy, after that Luke smiled at me a lot.'

'And then did you do anything?'

'I made lovely traily patterns in the sand and Daniel and I had a race to see who could build a sand castle quickest.'

'But then did you do anything?'

'At story time I was tired so I sat on Miss Howard's knee and the story was about a caterpillar and do you know Mummy, caterpillars turn into beautiful butterflies.'

'So, did you do anything today?'

'We sang Happy Birthday to Jack and counted the candles on his cake. Oh, and I helped Hannah find her coat because it was on the wrong peg so she was a bit upset.'

'But did you do anything today?'

'Well, when Mrs Crompton asked us to tidy up, I quickly painted you a picture, 'cos I knew you'd say, "What did you do at nursery today?"'

(Heard, 2003)

There is widespread acceptance that early childhood is an important time for children's learning and that what takes place during this period is not only of paramount importance in the child's development but also lays the foundation for lifelong learning (Anning and Edwards, 2006; Bruce, 2004; Fawcett, 2009; Fisher, 2002; Miller and Deveraux, 2003; Siraj-Blatchford and Clarke, 2000). Heard (2003) highlights the way in which children's learning can be outcome driven, not only by practitioners but also by society in general. There can be a disinterest in the process in the hurry to discover the outcome, yet it is the process of the learning experience that can be the most informative in relation to developing, sustaining and extending children's learning.

We have begun with Heard's poem because we think it is a great contrast to the monosyllabic response many children give when asked: 'What did you do today?' In our experience children often reply: 'Nothing', 'Do I have to?', 'I don't know' or 'I don't want to tell you!' This may be because children do not necessarily perceive that the outcome is more important than the process. This is an example of an adult-imposed construct of the response they would expect, i.e. the child telling them all about their day. Sometimes children may give a response in order to get something they want, such as 'I'll tell you if I can have a sweet'. This links to behavioural approaches found in many early years settings where children are rewarded for meeting adults' expectations: 'If you do your work-sheet then you can go and play', meaning 'If you don't do your worksheet you won't be able to play', thus embedding a culture of compliance in children.

Although Bruce (2004, p. 29) acknowledges 'because we think that children ought to learn something, it does not mean that we can make them learn it', we would suggest that compliance remains an implicit necessity for children's learning within the new EYFS. In contrast, Robinson and Aronica (2010) warns that an expectation of compliance as preparation for school readiness and employability can potentially damage children's love of learning and stifle their burgeoning interests and talents. Interestingly enough, there is a greater empha-sis on the need for school readiness in the new EYFS (DfE, 2012), despite con-cerns regarding what children are being prepared for. Robinson and Aronica (2010) suggests that very little has changed in terms of schooling since the beginning of the 20th century, despite an era of rapid changes making it difficult to predict what will be necessary for children to learn for the future. There is also further evidence that children are not necessarily ready at such a young age to be preparing for formal school (House, 2011).

There are parallels with Taguchi (2010, p. 17) in terms of a 'pre-decided' cur-riculum where the direction is 'vertical and hierarchical, with "the one who already knows" in a position over and above "the one who does not already know" and is to be educated'. These examples highlight the dichotomies between adults' thinking and children's thinking, and between process and outcome. Heard's poem suggests that young children are quite well aware of these and some will navigate them successfully and in the process will be able to develop a 'voice' within the parameters of the EYFS and the child's own cultural context. By this we mean the child's capacity and ability to understand and comply with adult expectations while being able to put forward their own interpretation of their experiences and ways of doing things.

In the review of the EYFS (Tickell, 2011) there were clear recommendations to reduce the number of learning outcomes from 69 to 17. There was also recogni-tion that practitioners are burdened with paperwork which takes them away from valuable time spent engaging with and listening to children. However, the philosophy that underpins the new EYFS continues to encourage the child to establish their individuality and identity as long as it 'fits in' with the age and stage requirements of the four themes: 'A unique child', 'Positive relationships',

'Enabling environments' and 'Children develop and learn in different ways and at different rates', which are set out in discrete compartments within the documentation (DfE, 2012). Although we recognise the constructive nature of this approach, which remains unchanged since 2008, this delineation of what is required is still at odds with the original spirit of the EYFS, which stated: 'Whatever children bring is an indication of their current interest and should be supported' (DCSF, 2008, p. 7).

There continues to be an apparent lack of trust in practitioners' ability to support children's learning and development without specific direction. This seems to be evident in the contradictory language used within the framework, which makes explicit that practitioners 'should' and 'must' deliver the required learning expectations of the curriculum. Similarly, the over-prescriptive ways in which children are required to meet the intended learning goals do not suggest a sense of trust in children's capacities and may even stifle the development of their cultural, social, emotional and intellectual capital. The unintended consequence of this is that the voice of the child may be 'silenced' through the interpretation and implementation of the EYFS. However,

> children show us they know how to walk along the path to understanding. Once children are helped to perceive themselves as authors or inventors, once they are helped to discover the pleasure of inquiry, their motivation and interest explode. The age of childhood, more than the ages that follow, is characterized by such expectations.
>
> (Malaguzzi, 1998, p. 67)

Embedded within the EYFS is an assumption that adults know what is best and how children should 'enjoy and achieve' (DfE, 2012) through the experiences they are offered. Adults tend to lead children down pathways rather than enabling the children to carve out their own because the EYFS lays the foundations for what children need to know and experience without the recognition that children know their own minds and have their own cultures.

The following example from practice highlights different competencies and capacities of young children as architects, authors and creators of their own learning and development. It is a reflection of the intentions that underpinned the EYFS (DCSF, 2008, p. 11) as a play-based curriculum where 'children are competent learners from birth and develop and learn in a wide variety of ways'. The approach of the practitioner has been to draw upon and support 'children's current interests' (DCSF, 2008).

Lily asked Karen to help her draw a rainbow with the chalks. They each chose different colours to draw the arcs. When they had drawn the rainbow, other children joined them to help (Robbie, Izzie, Harry, Millie and Ellie). Lily drew the sun, Karen began on the clouds, Harry drew a butterfly near the sun. Lily announced that they needed flowers. Izzie drew stems but left them; later Lily and Karen began the flowers. Robbie was right by Karen's side adding his part and saying how much he was enjoying it. There was a comfortable ease as children joined and left at various points. Similarly, Lily and Karen built the picture, Lily being very relaxed as to how it developed. There was a lot of laughter when Harry fell into the small empty sand tray at the edge of the drawing. Daniel and Robbie did the same and as the three sat where they landed, there was lots of laughter.

Later on Robbie asked Karen to help him draw a rainbow. Robbie wanted a picture of Karen and him and his family inside the rainbow (below). He drew all of his family and Anjali's family too. He made the heads, arms and legs. Robbie said he loved doing the chalks. At the end Robbie drew a line between Karen and him. Pausing to think about whether or not to ask Robbie about this, Karen asked what the line was for and he said, 'It's so no one can get us.' He added more lines over his family.

Meanwhile, the children had drawn a symbolic path to walk along. The line extended beyond the immediate drawing area. It appeared to have a definite start line and led to the rainbow. In contrast to the outcome-driven nature of

the EYFS, this was not a planned activity with a specific outcome because it was an open day for new children and families. However, the valuable learning that had taken place during this child-initiated, purposeful activity developed their interests as well as bringing together the children's complex experiences, feelings, thoughts and understandings.

Contemporary definitions of curriculum (Anning, 1998; Miller and Deveraux, 2003; Young, 1996) usually relate to the context in which learning is taking place. Although curricula often focus on planned activities designed to achieve particular developmental and educational aims, educationalists such as Blenkin and Kelly (1994) have called into question what is considered appropriate for inclusion in an early years curriculum. Recognition has been given that learning is contextual – 'children learn best from their own experiences' (Young, 1996, p. 19) – and that young children's learning needs change as their development progresses.

According to David (2001, p. 56), 'the fundamental building blocks of a curriculum can be seen as the knowledge (facts), skills, concepts/understandings and attitudes to be acquired'. This is a much broader definition and indicates that the curriculum can be delivered anywhere the child is, whether at home or in an early years setting. It implies that the curriculum is about more than knowledge and skills; it includes a 'hidden curriculum' from which children learn social skills, attitudes and behaviours.

The EYFS encouraged practitioners to recognise the importance of listening to the choices and decisions that children make (DCSF, 2008, p. 26). In practice this may not be straightforward, since the subjective perspectives of adults and children may be different, as the following example demonstrates.

Sujey, aged 2, was in the bookshop with her aunt, waiting for her mother to arrive. They were looking at books together. Sujey selected a book from the bottom shelf and sat on the floor to look at it. The book was about witches and it was very dark in colour. Sujey's aunt found a colourful book and showed it to Sujey, swapping it with the book about witches, which she replaced on the shelf. Sujey looked at the colourful book for about two minutes, then placed it on the floor next to her. She reached for the book about witches, which had been replaced on the shelf, and began looking through the pages. Sujey continued looking at the book for the next 15 minutes until her mother arrived. She seemed absolutely engrossed in it.

Sujey's aunt asked if she would like her to buy the colourful book, which was still lying next to Sujey on the floor. Sujey stood up and said that she wanted the book about witches. Although her aunt couldn't really understand what Sujey liked about the book, she agreed to get it for her. It was important to recognise that Sujey was developing her autonomy and learning to express her choice and to know that this is valued.

Although the EYFS encourages practitioners to support the decisions that children make (DCSF, 2008, p. 27), the ways in which materials are offered to them will invariably influence their decision making. These may be quite subtle cues, such as tone of voice, facial expression or gesture that indicates the adult's perception of what they think the child will enjoy. Although practitioners would like to think they encourage children to make their own decisions, they do not necessarily recognise the extent to which young children have the capacity to participate in decisions that affect them (Miller, 2003). This may be one of the reasons why the concept of adults listening to young children does not have prominence in the new EYFS (DfE, 2012). Instead, there seems to be an emphasis on making sure children listen.

When adults influence choices for children there is potentially a danger of ~
ing out on how much young children can tell us about their ·
their learning and development that they have achieved throu
of learning experiences. David (2001) also suggests that differen·

have differing expectations of their children, and these are imposed on them from an early age, in an unwritten curriculum. This therefore suggests that whichever curriculum is employed needs to retain cultural diversity. It is important to recognise that different types of curricula have different purposes, which are 'underpinned by different values and principles and are informed by different assumptions and beliefs about children' (David, 2001, p. 59). The early years curriculum in Turkey also has an emphasis on learning and development but aims to facilitate children's and families' participation in the learning journey. It has been influenced by the early years curricula in Reggio Emilia and views 'creativity as a social good' (Banaji et al., 2006, p. 24) to be embraced collectively by the whole community.

In one of the nurseries that we visited in Ankara, for children aged 3–6, the large entrance hall is viewed as an important social space which facilitates the interaction of children, parents and practitioners. The walls are covered with interesting things for the children to look at, and there are pictures of their work and examples of what they have said. One question they have been asked is: 'What is a human?' The children's answers, including 'I don't know but I am one', are written down by the staff and put on the wall.

Children learn spelling by another technique, using words attached to parachutes, which are placed at the top of the notice board. As time goes by and the children learn the words, they are moved down the board and new ones take their place. This therefore caters for all the children – those who grasp words quickly and those who take a little more time, thus mirroring the EYFS principle of learning and development which 'recognises that children learn and develop in different ways and at different rates' (DfE, 2012, p. 3).

The EYFS has developed from the Foundation Stage Curriculum, a centralised curriculum framework that provided guidance to early childhood practitioners and teachers to enable them to prepare children for the next stage of schooling. It was defined as 'everything children do, see, hear, or feel in their setting, both planned and unplanned' (QCA, 2000, p. 1). The curriculum promoted learning and development through the use of learning goals and stepping stones, thus indicating that the Foundation Stage was based on a developmental model dominated by the theories of developmental psychology (David et al., 2000). The guidance to the Foundation Stage recognised that children develop through certain stages, hence the stepping stones, but it stated that not all children will follow them in a particular sequence, and that all children would move along them at different rates (QCA, 2000, p. 27). It therefore recognised children as individuals who had different experiences in their childhood before starting the Foundation Stage, which would affect their development.

Using a similar approach, the EYFS combined Birth to Three Matters, the Curriculum Guidance for the Foundation Stage and the National Standards for Under 8s' Daycare and Childminding into one coherent framework, which was underpinned by the Government's key policy 'Every Child Matters'. There is an emphasis on linking the child's home experiences with their experiences in the early years setting. This reflects a shift in the government's approach to children and families and the recognition that the wellbeing of children and families needs to be given a higher priority with greater investment. Children's development is viewed holistically and much more broadly than merely as a preparation for school, while recognising the value of capacities already developed from birth to three.

In the 2008 EYFS, 'the overarching aim of the EYFS was to help young children achieve the five Every Child Matters outcomes of staying safe, being healthy, enjoying and achieving, making a positive contribution, and achieving economic well-being' (DCSF, 2008, p. 7). This theme continues in the new EYFS with the aim 'to ensure that children learn and develop well and are kept healthy and safe' (DfE, 2012, p. 2).

Despite an attempt to view children more holistically, ongoing assessment is still seen as 'an integral part of the learning and development process' (DfE, 2012, p. 10). Observations of the child are matched to the early learning goals using 13 sets of assessment scales, although it was never intended that these should be used as a checklist (Beckley et al., 2009). The EYFS profile provides a record of the child's learning and achievements which may be shared between parents and practitioners, and may be used to support the child's learning and development. However, the continued move towards the requirement of academic goals for very young children, in the EYFS, remains of great concern to many early years educators (Nutbrown, 2011). The focus of this concern is that the attempt to meet assessment outcomes may inhibit rather than encourage young children's autonomy, creativity and sense of mastery, and may indeed be a contributory factor to England's persistent record of under-achievement (Nutbrown, 2011), for example, with the over-prescription in relation to language, literacy and numeracy.

The following example from practice exemplifies a preoccupation with assessing progress in literacy and numeracy rather than tuning into the child's interests.

Under the cover of a green army camouflage canopy, staff had set out a large tray with lots of plastic minibeasts, leaves, logs, butterflies, magnifying glasses and information books. There was an array of texts stapled on the wall with photos and information about the minibeasts. Harry was looking at minibeasts through a magnifying glass. One by one he examined them in his hand, holding the magnifying glass at varying distances from the bug. 'This one's got spots on,' he said. 'One, two, three, four, five, six.'

Harry took the small ladybird over to a nearby table. The table had been set out previously with Eric Carle mini stories, *The Very Hungry Caterpillar* and the foods he eats in the story, cloth butterflies of different sizes which to adult eyes looked appealing and related to other activities in the nursery. However, Harry cleared his own space in the middle of this. As he carefully placed the bug on the green cloth, he announced that the ladybird was going in his workshop. One by one he went back and forth from the workshop to the tray, each time carefully examining an assortment of bugs until he had a collection of them in his workshop. He carefully set them down one at a time in a horizontal row until the practitioner approached the area and said, 'Come on Harry, come and do your number line.'

What the teacher had not recognised was that Harry was engaged in a highly creative literacy and numeracy activity which was meeting the requirements of the curriculum. Unlike successful systems in other countries, which move children slowly from the concrete and representational, with the focus on developing confidence in spoken language, the English system moves quickly into abstract letters and words. This does not support evidence from research that children cannot develop a capacity to think at abstract levels unless the tasks presented to them are embedded in contexts which make sense to them on an everyday concrete level (Donaldson, 1978; Kress, 1997; Whitehead, 1990).

Harry had constructed a creative activity that enabled him to develop representational thinking from a concrete context which could have been developed further by the teacher. Taking Harry away to do an abstract numeracy activity missed the opportunity for the practitioner to sustain and extend Harry's knowledge and understanding, as well as being a missed opportunity for the teacher to observe and learn more about Harry than through his 'number line'.

Despite being interrupted in what he was engrossed in and being moved to another area of the nursery, Harry managed to cope with the unexpected transition to meet the expectations of the teacher. Whereas brighter children and those from more privileged backgrounds may cope with these demands, less culturally competent children, in an education context, could lose confidence and might never recover (Anning and Edwards, 1999).

Tom, who had been identified as potentially needing language support, had chosen a pale skin colour to represent himself on his Father's Day card. Next to him was his father, whom he coloured in green. When the teacher walked past, she said, 'Why is your Daddy green, Tom? Is he an alien?' Tom had no answer to this bewildering question, but it could potentially have influenced his pride in what he had created.

There remains an implicit assumption in the EYFS that there is a level playing field for all children in the way that it suggests leaders will be able to 'ignite (sic) children's curiosity and enthusiasm for learning, and for building their capacity to learn' (DfE, 2012, p. 4). Similarly, in 'inclusive practices that promote and value diversity and difference' (DfE, 2012, p. 26), there is also an assumption that all children bring with them the necessary social and cultural capital to respond similarly to the learning opportunities provided. There is no acknowledgement that children bring differing levels of social and cultural capital and that one's cultural identity can be shaped by, and can shape, other cultural identities. In reality, some cultural identities, such as the middle class in England, are more powerful than others and can therefore become more dominant. In a similar way, giving individuals a right to their culture does not, by itself, ensure cultural diversity. Practitioners need to recognise that within cultural groups there are also differences, depending on individuals' experiences (Ang, 2010).

Cousins (1999, p. 10) writes evocatively about four-year-old Sonnyboy, who could be considered at a social and cultural disadvantage because of his background, but has the capacity to 'jolt adults into thinking'. Sonnyboy questions 'irritating interruptions' with, 'why'd'you interrupt us so?' For example, on hearing the bell at playtime, he said, 'That don't make no sense . . . I just got to the interesting bit. I don't care about the time, that's plain stupid . . . time's as long as it takes' (Cousins, 1999, p. 36).

Fear of interruption stops children from choosing or starting some activities. This doesn't relate only to specific activities, it can also relate to the child's creativity, disposition and 'threads of thinking' (Nutbrown, 2011). Learning can be extended differently depending on the time and context. The themes, ideas, interests and interpretations will vary for different children at different times.

The children were writing (structured activity) at the table. Mia began to move from side to side in her seat. 'Conga, conga, conga . . .' she sang. Mia stopped writing, stood up and danced the conga around the classroom, singing as she went. Her teacher made her a sticker with a smiley face on it and the words, 'I am the Conga Queen!' Later Mia said she just felt like doing the conga.

As a practitioner it is important, in order to develop, sustain and extend children's learning, to recognise that differences can be complex and that learning doesn't happen in a linear way (Nutbrown, 2011). In the EYFS there appears to be an emphasis on products and progression rather than on using children's interests and capacities to facilitate continuity of learning and the development of themes that important and relevant to children.

Sujey was an avid reader from an early age. Her reading ability was noted as excellent by her class teacher. All the children in the class were asked to keep a reading record book. They were told to read a passage from their current book (the amount depended on reading ability) and then analyse what they had read. Instead of developing her reading skills, reading became a chore for Sujey. Although she didn't mind the exercise at the beginning, the continual analysis started to interrupt her reading pattern and, more importantly, her enjoyment of the texts themselves. She read less and was not inclined to do the 'homework'.

One weekend she unintentionally left the reading record with her aunt, who lived far from her. Sujey's mother and aunt discussed this and decided that the record was inhibiting her reading and her enjoyment. Sujey's mother spoke with her teacher, who agreed that Sujey would not have to keep a reading record for the next week or so. Sujey started reading again with the enjoyment she had always shown. She did not keep a reading record again and no one mentioned that she should.

This example demonstrates how interpreting the curriculum also has an impact on the role of the practitioner as early years carer and educator. Abbott (2001, p. 70) describes this as the difference between teaching and learning. By setting out areas of learning and learning goals that the teachers have to work towards helping the children to achieve, there is a risk that the EYFS can become prescriptive unless there is an appreciation of children's individual differences. The way the EYFS is structured, with assessed outcomes, lessens opportunities for practitioners to evaluate their observations of children using prior knowledge and experience. This, in effect, may lead to practitioners feeling deskilled. Having to conform to a set of standards may in turn make them less likely to recognise children's individual competencies and capabilities.

This potential deskilling of the practitioner has implications for workforce development, training and qualifications. 'The evidence is clear on how a well-qualified and appropriately skilled early years workforce makes a real difference to the quality of provision and outcomes for young children' (Tickell, 2011, p. 42). Eaude (2011) suggests that pedagogically there is currently an emphasis on the transfer of knowledge rather than the development of children's thinking. In order to facilitate this approach to the learning process, practitioners need to be reflective and have good knowledge and understanding of research and underpinning theoretical perspectives (Duffy, 2010).

Without this knowledge and understanding there is the risk of a shift in the perceived priorities of the way in which children's learning and development can be supported. The following example demonstrates how by focusing on one practicality, a practitioner, acting as a mentor, missed the richness of a learning opportunity and failed to recognise and acknowledge the student's good practice.

Sharaz, an undergraduate at the end of his second year, was nervous about being observed by his tutor. He planned a creative painting activity with small groups of children. Not all the children wanted to be involved in the activity, but Sharaz started off with a group of four. One of the nursery staff was also sitting at the table with Sharaz and the children.

Sharaz facilitated the activity well and encouraged the children to mix the paints and combine colours as they wished. Sammy, aged 4, wanted to do more mixing than painting, so Sharaz allowed him to do this for a couple of minutes before encouraging him to put brush to paper. Sammy painted for a few minutes, using several different colours. When Sharaz asked him what the picture was meant to be, Sammy said he did not know but he liked the colours. After another minute of mixing more colours, Sammy decided to paint over what he had done with the colour black. The practitioner said, 'Oh, Sammy, now you have spoilt your picture.' Sammy looked surprised and replied, 'No, I haven't.' He got up from the table, leaving his picture behind. Sharaz asked if he would like to take the painting home. Sammy said yes and Sharaz wrote his name on the painting.

Janice, who previously had not wanted to do the painting activity, took Sammy's place at the table. She eagerly started mixing paints and putting brush strokes on the paper. Sharaz was praising her, as he had done with all the children. He suddenly realised that Janice was not wearing a waterproof apron. He gently encouraged Janice to put one on, although it took some time for her to comply with the request. At the end of the activity, when the practitioner was giving feedback to Sharaz, the first thing she said was that Sharaz must always make sure that the children were wearing aprons before allowing them to paint.

Although it is important to ensure that the children's clothing is protected when carrying out 'messy' activities, the focus on feedback should have been the way in which Sharaz had developed the activity in response to the children's pathways to understanding. He encouraged the children to have the space to make their decisions. He understood that Sammy was enjoying the process of mixing the paints together rather than being concerned with the final outcome or product of the painting. This is another good example of the difference in perception between the child and the vocationally qualified practitioner (NVQ3), where there is a tension between process and outcome. The focus on the practicalities may have been because the practitioner did not recognise the depth and richness of the learning taking place in the development of the children and Sharaz.

his is not to say that qualified teachers do not miss these highly meaningful
:arning opportunities, as they are often constrained by extraneous influences,
vhether internal or external.

The children were sitting four at a table in the Reception class, busy drawing
and colouring. The teacher and teaching assistant were going round the tables
discussing the drawings with the children. Alice was drawing some flowers. She
was colouring the leaves purple. The teacher told Alice she was using the wrong
colour and that she should use green. When the teacher was asked why she had
encouraged Alice to change the colour she was using without discussing it, as
this seemed to diminish Alice's creative actions, the teacher replied that it was
the parents who would have complained that their children were not drawing
and colouring properly.

Alderson (2003) questions the value and purpose of schooling and the extent to
which children shape or are shaped by societal needs and expectations. The
findings in a recent evaluation of practitioners' experiences of implementing
EYFS (Brooker *et al.*, 2010) suggested that practitioners considered it to be
highly influential in their practice and welcomed the 'play-based and child-led
framework' of EYFS. They felt it was more appropriate for the learning and
development of young children than the previous frameworks, which were
focused more on children's 'preparation' for school. In principle, they thought
that the areas of learning were appropriate and that the EYFS encouraged a better partnership with parents. However, there were causes for concern from
some of the practitioners' responses. These included the potential labelling of
children rather than celebration of the 'Unique Child'; the level of assessment
required which did not necessarily reflect the real learning and development of
the children in all types of settings; the difference in the interpretation and
implementation of the assessment practices themselves; the relationship
between parents and practitioners; and the 'significant variations' in the education and training of professionals and practitioners, which influenced the way
in which the EYFS was interpreted and implemented.

> There is so much pressure on parents and practitioners to follow approved
> procedures and meet targets that we can get sidetracked into focusing on
> young children's skills and capabilities rather than on the child themselves.
> (Morton, 2009, p. 42)

Through the entrance hall of the Ankara nursery there are two displays – work
done by the children at home with their families, based on an identified theme.
There are other ways in which parents are included in their child's experience of
nursery. The parents write notes for their children and put them in a box so that
the children have a strong link between home and the setting.

The concept of a 'Unique Child' within the EYFS encourages practitioners to focus on what children should be doing at a particular time in a particular context. McDowall Clark (2010, p. 46) suggests that practitioners should consider the curriculum as a 'dynamic process rather than as expectations to be met'. Despite the rhetoric of supporting a 'Unique Child', the EYFS may be interpreted as portraying the 'Homogenous Child' that has access to high-quality, ideal environments with ample resources, which in itself is questionable. There is a danger of the child being homogenised in the rhetoric of the 'overarching principles' (DfE, 2012, p. 3) of the EYFS, which seeks to 'achieve' the five outcomes put forward by Every Child Matters, without recognising that children do not have similar equality of opportunity to high-quality learning environments. The aspirational policy outcomes of 'staying safe', 'being healthy', 'enjoying and achieving', 'making a positive contribution' and 'achieving economic wellbeing' lack an agreed definition on their meaning in the context of children's lived experiences. There remains an emphasis on the adult's interpretation of what children are doing rather than the facilitation of the children's own reflections and interpretations of their learning and development.

In the Ankara nursery, children are given the opportunity to reflect on and learn about themselves and the world around them. In one activity the children were asked to decide collectively what was important to them. They needed to come up with one thing once a day for 100 days and pictorial representations would be placed on the wall each day. The children chose things such as family, friends, sleep, food, etc. On the 100th day the choice was 'surprises'.

The nursery children are also introduced to democratic decision making. Each week the children have to vote on an issue by using ballot boxes. One week it was which cake they should have that Friday and another week it was which new logo should be used for the setting. In each case the children were given three choices. These approaches to learning help give children a sense of real participation and completion. By being allowed the time to complete an activity, all children are motivated to engage with further pursuits.

This is in contrast to the EYFS, which encourages practitioners to work towards more rigid timelines for the children to meet the numerous curriculum requirements. In the hurry to achieve numerous outcomes, the EYFS has the potential to develop into what Dadds (2002) refers to as the 'Hurry-along' curriculum. When there isn't enough time for children to complete what they want to, an important sense of achievement is lacking. This can potentially lead to children being demotivated if they do not believe they will meet the required learning outcomes, and thus developing a self-fulfilling prophecy of 'learning to be stupid' (Holt, 1995).

Despite the good intentions of the EYFS there remains a great disparity in how it is being interpreted and implemented. From the examples discussed in this chapter it can be seen that different interpretations either encourage or stifle children's learning and development. Concerns remain over the prescriptive nature of the EYFS. In reality, it does not support true partnerships based on dialogue and mutual interests between children, families and settings. There is still an assumption that children need to learn from adults rather than adults learning from observations of children and through listening to their discussions. The intrinsic nature of play still needs to be recognised as an excellent source for children's learning and development. Rather than developing activities to meet the requirements of the curriculum, it may be more beneficial for practitioners to look at what the child is doing and then see how the children's own constructs meet the necessary requirements.

It is not always necessary to use assessment pro formas when observing children. It may be more effective to observe the children on a number of occasions in different contexts before making decisions about their developmental capabilities. This approach facilitates knowledge and understanding about children in a much more holistic way. This can enable the practitioner to recognise what children themselves contribute to the learning process, which can help them to better understand, support and scaffold children's learning and development. It can be easy to forget that if they are enjoying what they are doing and it is fun, they will want to learn. Children really do know their own minds!

Reflective Questions

1. How can listening to and observing children help to 'capture the moments' which can become the missed opportunities? Why might this be challenging?

2. How can the EYFS help to connect creativity with social empowerment?

3. Why has House (2011) described the EYFS as being 'too much, too soon' in the push towards children's readiness for school?

4. How can children's and families' diverse linguistic, cultural and socio-economic backgrounds be embraced by the EYFS?

5. Why is it important for professionals and practitioners to develop their understanding and interpretation of the EYFS through continuing professional development?

References

Abbott, L. (2001) *Differentiation in Teaching and Learning: Aspirations and reality in primary education*, University of Ulster.

Alderson, P. (2003) *Institutional Rites and Rights: A century of childhood*, London: Institute of Education.

Ang, L. L. Y. (2010) 'Critical perspectives on cultural diversity in early childhood: building an inclusive curriculum and provision', *Early Years: An International Journal of Research and Development*, 30(1), 41–52.

Anning, A. (1998) 'Appropriateness or effectiveness in the early childhood curriculum in the UK: some research evidence', *International Journal of Early Years Education*, 6(3), 299–314.

Anning, A. and Edwards, A. (1999) *Promoting Learning from Birth to Five: Developing Professional Practice in the Pre-school*. Buckingham: Open University Press.

Anning, A. and Edwards, A. (2006) *Promoting Learning from Birth to Five: Developing professional practice in the pre-school* (2nd Edition), Buckingham: Open University Press.

Banaji, S., Burn, A. and Buckingham, D. (2006) *The Rhetorics of Creativity: A review of the literature*, London: Creative Partnerships, Arts Council England.

Beckley, P., Elvidge, K. and Hendry, H. (2009) *Implementing the Early Years Foundation Stage: A handbook*, Maidenhead: Open University Press.

Blenkin, G. M. and Kelly, A. V. (1994) *Early Childhood Education: A developmental curriculum*, London: Paul Chapman.

Brooker, L., Rogers, S., Ellis, D., Hallet, E. and Roberts-Holmes, G. (2010) *Practitioners' Experiences of the Early Years Foundation Stage*, Nottingham: DCSF Publications.

Bruce, T. (2004) *Developing Learning in Early Childhood*, London: Sage.

Cousins, J. (1999) *Listening to Four Year Olds. How they help us plan their education and care*, London: National Early Years Network.

Dadds, M. (2002) 'The "hurry-along" curriculum', in Pollard, A. (2002) *Readings for Reflective Teaching*, London: Continuum.

David, T. (ed.) (2001) *International Advances in Applied Early Education Volume 1. Promoting evidence-based practice in early childhood education: research and its implications*, London: JAI.

David, T., Thompson, L. and Aubrey, A. (eds.) (2000) *Early Childhood Educational Research: Issues in methodology and ethics*, London: Routledge.

Department for Children, Schools and Families (DCSF) (2008) *The Early Years Foundation Stage: Setting the standards for learning, development and care for children from birth to five*, Nottingham: DCSF Publications.

Department for Education (DfE) (2012) *Statutory Framework for the Early Years Foundation Stage: Setting the standards for learning, development and care for children from birth to five*. Available online at: www.education.gov.uk/publications/standard/AllPublications/Page1/DFE-00023-2012.

Donaldson, M. (1978) *Children's Minds*, London: Fontana Press.

Duffy, B. (2010) 'The early years curriculum', in Pugh, G. and Duffy, B. (eds.) *Contemporary Issues in the Early Years*, London: Sage.

Eaude, T. (2011) *Thinking Through Pedagogy for Primary and Early Years*, Exeter: Learning Matters.

Fawcett, M. (2009) *Learning Through Child Observation* (2nd Edition), London: Jessica Kingsley Publishers.

Fisher, J. (2002) *Starting from the Child*, Buckingham: Oxford University Press.

Heard, S. (2003) 'And what did you do at pre-school today?' *Nursery World*. Available online at: www.nurseryworld.co.uk/news/717401/pre-school-today/.

Holt, J. (1995) *How Children Learn*, Volume 1983, Part 3, Boston, MA: Addison Wesley Publishing.

House, R. (2011) *Too Much, Too Soon? Early learning and the erosion of childhood*, Stroud: Hawthorn Press.

Kress, G. (1997) *Before Writing: Rethinking the paths to literacy*, London: Routledge.

Malaguzzi, L. (1998) 'History, ideas and basic philosophy: an interview with Lella Gandini', in Edwards, E., Gandini, L. and Forman, G. (eds.) *The Hundred Languages of Children: The Reggio Emilia approach – advanced reflections*, Greenwich, CT: Alex Publishing Corporation.

McDowall Clark, R. (2010) *Childhood in Society for Early Childhood Studies*, Exeter: Learning Matters.

Miller, J. (2003) *Never Too Young. How young children can take responsibility and make decisions*, London: Save the Children Fund.

Miller, L. and Deveraux, L. (2003) *Supporting Children's Learning in the Early Years*, London: David Fulton Publishers.

Morton, D. (2009) 'Developing appreciation of babies' and young children's behaviour. Why do they do what they do?' in Fabian, H. and Mould, C., *Development & Learning for Very Young Children*, London: Sage.

Nutbrown, C. (2011) *Threads of Thinking Schemas and Young Children's Learning* (4th Edition), London: Sage.

Qualifications and Curriculum Authority (QCA) (2000) *Curriculum Guidance for the Foundation Stage*, Sheffield: QCA Publications.

Robinson, K. and Aronica, L. (2010) *The Element: How finding your passion changes everything*, London: Penguin Books.

Siraj-Blatchford, I. and Clarke, P. (2000) *Supporting Identity, Diversity & Language in the Early Years (Supporting Early Learning)*, Buckingham: Oxford University Press.

Taguchi, H. L. (2010) 'Rethinking pedagogical practices in early childhood education: a multidimensional approach to learning and inclusion', in Yelland, N. (ed.) *Contemporary Perspectives on Early Childhood Education*, Maidenhead: Open University Press.

Tickell, C. (2011) *The Early Years: Foundations for life, health and learning.* An independent report on the Early Years Foundation Stage to Her Majesty's Government, Nottingham: DfE.

Whitehead, M. (1990) *Language and Literacy in the Early Years*, London: Sage.

Young, M. (1996) *Early Childhood Development: Investing in the future*, Washington, DC: The World Bank.

3

The challenges of implementing an early years curriculum: a practitioner's perspective

Ruksana Mohammed

Overview

The *Early Years Foundation Stage* (EYFS) (DfE, 2012) is a statutory curriculum framework for all early years settings in England that cater for children aged zero to five years. Although there are varying opinions on the content of the document itself, no one can deny that it has been formed on the belief of achieving better outcomes for young children through quality experiences and approaches initiated by the adults they come into contact with. The purpose of this chapter is to explore the daily issues and challenges facing the early years workforce that have been brought about by the implementation of the EYFS curriculum in their practice. Key issues and challenges that will be addressed are the interpretation of the EYFS into practice; the operational challenges that hinder the requirements of key areas of the EYFS; challenges in the provision of a learning environment that addresses the EYFS; the belief system of practitioners that conflict when working with the EYFS; and finally the need for time to effectively interpret, deliver and maintain an early years curriculum.

Key Themes

- Implementing the Early Years Foundation Stage (EYFS).
- Issues and challenges in delivering the EYFS.
- The role of practitioners and student practitioners in interpreting and implementing the curriculum.

Introduction

Over the last decade, there has been significant government emphasis on the quality of the workforce in early childhood education and care in the United Kingdom, with an understanding that quality outcomes for young children include a need for a highly skilled workforce (David, 2004). The government emphasises the need for 'a workforce that is competent and capable of delivering the requirements for regulation' (Musgrave, 2010, p. 435).

One such regulation requirement is the delivery of the EYFS, a statutory curriculum framework for children aged zero to five years. The overarching aim of the EYFS is to help young children achieve the five Every Child Matters (ECM) (DfES, 2004) outcomes of staying safe, being healthy, enjoying and achieving, making a positive contribution, and achieving economic wellbeing. This is achieved through 'setting the standards' for the learning, development and care that children 'should' experience when attending an early years setting. The EYFS further confirms that 'quality learning experiences for children requires a quality workforce' (DfE, 2012, p. 7).

The EYFS as a 'guidance for practitioners' is informed by theories, philosophies, values and beliefs of what young children 'should' and 'must' learn and the 'levels of development that most children can be expected to reach by the age of five' (DfE, 2011, p. 1). The framework further 'specifies requirements for learning and development' (DfE, 2012, p. 2) for the early childhood practitioner in emphasising the 'must' of what they 'should' be doing to 'shape activities and experiences for children' (ibid). These are mainly to achieve the ECM outcomes as well as the pre-determined, assessable outcomes stated in the seven areas of learning and development of the EYFS 'that providers *must* help children to work towards' (DfE, 2012, p. 4). Yet in reality the challenges of curriculum implementation are tested and stretched in the day-to-day practical realities of practitioners working in a setting.

Early childhood practitioners play a significant role in the interpretation, delivery and maintaining of the curriculum. However, there has been a continual change in the curriculum in England since the launch of the first desirable outcomes in 1996. More recently, with the Tickell Review (2011), the EYFS once again, three years after its introduction in 2008, changed for September 2012. Yet despite the complexity of the work of practitioners, within challenging early years contexts, there has been no period of consolidation during which practitioners can implement, develop and take ownership of the EYFS, before it possibly changes again. Urban (2008, p. 136) quite rightly states that in the implementation of any curriculum:

> The dilemma unfolds between the day-to-day experience of having to act concretely, spontaneously and autonomously in ever-changing, uncertain situations which, to a large extent, are determined by factors beyond the practitioners' control.

As this chapter will show, practitioners experience daily challenges in implementing the early years curriculum. Vignettes from practice will aim to contextualise the environment and context in which early childhood practitioners

Vignette 1

Case study of a student practitioner's experience in working with the EYFS

Nicola, a second-year student on an Early Childhood Studies degree, is required to observe a play activity in a setting that implements the EYFS and then to map this to the areas of learning and development stated in the EYFS. When discussing her learning with her tutor, Nicola reveals that she was experiencing difficulties in doing this. She states that there is too much content and she doesn't know where to start looking, and that she seems to have this problem at work all the time. The tutor puts away the EYFS document and asks Nicola to explain what her interpretation of the observation is, in her own words. Nicola fluently describes the learning and development taking place, as the tutor writes this down. The tutor then brings back the EYFS and asks Nicola to find in the practice guidance milestones/goals that best represent the thoughts and ideas she has just described and what she could do to take the children forward.

operate and how this tests the function and impact of the EYFS. The aim is to bring to the forefront the tension that exists between the document as a framework and the document in practice. The focus of this chapter is on the practitioners in their work with the EYFS rather than upon child outcomes. The term 'early childhood practitioner' will be used to refer to all those who work with young children, whatever their qualification route or training experience.

The EYFS guides the role of practitioners in supporting children's learning and development. In order to achieve this, Nicola (Vignette 1) is clearly reflecting and attempting to make sense of the observations she has collected. However, interpreting the observations in the context of the EYFS is proving challenging for Nicola, which then brings into question the notion of 'effective practice' or rather 'pedagogy' in curriculum delivery, which is clearly missing from the EYFS. Watkins and Mortimer (1999) explain pedagogy to be 'any conscious activity by one person designed to enhance learning in another'. The tutor was able to demonstrate this in the way in which she facilitated Nicola's understanding in the use of the EYFS. However, Nicola, without the support of the tutor, was not able to do the same for the children in 'closely matching what they [the practitioner] provide to children's current needs [the observation]' (Development Matters, 2012, p. 3). This questions what effective pedagogy, or rather the term 'practice' that the EYFS uses, actually entails in the delivery of the curriculum, and challenges how practitioners interpret the term 'effective practice'.

The *Study of Pedagogical Effectiveness in Early Learning* (SPEEL) (Moyles *et al.*, 2002), which aimed to identify characteristics of effective pedagogy in the early years, sets out the main characteristic of practitioners as being 'effective'. The 2008 EYFS further built on this by citing 'knowledgeable' adults (DCSF, 2008). Building on Musgrave's earlier notion of 'competent', the *Study on Competence Requirements in Early Childhood Education and Care* (CoRe) further highlights 'competence' as a 'characteristic of the entire early childhood system' (Urban *et al.*, 2011, p. 21). The current EYFS uses the term 'skilled staff' (DfE, 2012, p. 7) that are needed in delivering quality experiences to young children. This makes it clear not only that the role of the adult in children's care, learning and development is vital, but that effective practice/pedagogy requires practitioners to be 'effective' in what they do and how they do it, 'knowledgeable' in the various ways children learn and develop, and 'competent and skilled' in their specialist practice that supports quality experiences and outcomes for young children. However, the effectiveness, knowledge, competence and skills of early childhood practitioners are guided by the EYFS framework, which is endangered by misunderstanding or misinterpreting the framework, but is also challenged and stretched in the complex work of practitioners, as demonstrated in Nicola's experience.

Nicola has been in practice for seven years in her local early years setting, during which the EYFS has changed twice. She has demonstrated that she is a 'knowledgeable' and 'skilled' practitioner in her descriptions and interpretation of her observations. However, the in-depth content of the EYFS makes Nicola question her abilities in interpreting her observations to ensure 'competent' and 'effective' practice with the children. This concern is not a new one, but is ongoing for adults working with young children. The detailed framework of 2008 appeared daunting, with 'too much content', and could be the very reason practitioners actually refrained from engaging with it. Although the 2008 EYFS included Principles into Practice cards to ensure 'effective' practice, it is quite clear that Nicola, and very likely other practitioners like her, engaged with the document only for a time-consuming, detailed mapping of children's progression and not as a tool to support their existing skills and effective, knowledgeable and competent practice/pedagogy in the delivery of the curriculum.

Within higher education, the Early Childhood Studies degree advocates a holistic approach to children's learning and development. Nicola being asked to map the observation to the EYFS actually contradicts this approach as she is being asked to compartmentalise aspects of children's learning into set areas. Without the tutor's support, Nicola may not be able to understand that although she has mapped progression into separate areas, they actually intertwine and therefore are of a holistic nature, as one observation cannot ever demonstrate one area of learning or development. However, this support is often lacking in a practice setting, where practitioners are limited in understanding their roles in the implementation of the curriculum, but also where there is the issue of time and space.

These complex circumstances almost limit practitioner confidence, thinking, 'professional autonomy and interpretational skills' (Horvath, 2011, p. 2) to deliver an effective curriculum. Oberhuemer (2005) further argues that prior to government guidelines, the early childhood curriculum had professional autonomy, with practitioners making decisions about practice. She believes that while having regulations and standards should improve early childhood status, practitioners being asked to adhere to a prescribed framework could undermine their professional autonomy. This results in policy makers having more control, which then conflicts with the ideologies on care, learning, development and play, and in turn challenges effective practice.

The revised 2012 EYFS hopes to address these issues that practitioners such as Nicola are faced with. The emphasis was on the importance of simplifying the 2008 EYFS to make it even more accessible for practitioners. In order to do this, the 69 learning goals, mapped under six areas of learning and development, have been reduced to 17 under seven areas known as 'prime' and 'specific'.

The aim is to make the framework 'easy to access, understand and navigate', and to free the workforce from unnecessary paperwork and procedures, so that they can spend more time interacting with the children (Tickell, 2011). This may be a welcome change for practitioners such as Nicola, in gaining more autonomy, creativity and flexibility in the interpretation, delivery and maintaining of the curriculum, but will it support effective, knowledgeable, skilled and competent practice in challenging contexts in what a quality curriculum for children should look like?

As the EYFS states within its text, the assessment against the EYFS 'should not entail prolonged breaks from interaction with children, nor require excessive paperwork. Paperwork should be limited' (DfE, 2012, p. 10). Yet the curriculum begins: 'The learning and development requirements are given force by an Order made under section 39(1)(a) of the Childcare Act 2006' (DfE, 2012, p. 1).

It is compulsory to follow the EYFS, but in order to prove that it is being followed, practitioners like Nicola will need evidence, and evidence is always through paperwork. The Office for Standards in Education (Ofsted) carries out inspections of early years settings against the EYFS and reports on the quality and standards of provision. This very often requires a paper trail to illustrate how the setting ensures children meet the learning and development requirements of the EYFS, how they are assessed and what the setting does to support children. What the new EYFS has failed to address is the allocation of time to do this. Early childhood practitioners need time for assessment, which requires breaks from the children, in order to understand observations and then to move forward in the next steps for children's learning and development. The EYFS further has failed to clarify that if it requires early childhood practitioners to refrain from unnecessary paperwork, will Ofsted be advised to review its inspection regime in light of this?

Further interpretation issues lay within the text of the EYFS itself. The EYFS states that all areas of learning and development must be delivered through 'planned, purposeful play, with a balance of adult-led and child-initiated activities' (DfE, 2012, p. 6), i.e. the requirements of the EYFS are to be framed around play-based activities. Here there is a tension evident in the EYFS which highlights the extent to which the framework is open to interpretation. Tovey (2007) argues that the idea of play being 'planned for' and 'purposeful' is in tension with the definition of play being 'spontaneous', 'child initiated', which the EYFS advocates, and sometimes 'purposeless'. Here there is a remarkable difference between controlling and directing play so that it is deemed to be 'purposeful', and then observing play to identify what children can do, their talents and interests, and building on these in terms of shaping the curriculum. This then contradicts the balance of adult-led and child-initiated activities. What is the balance? How does one achieve this balance? How is this balance translated in practice? Swarbrick (2007, p. 117) argues that practitioners get a directive from the EYFS that play should underpin delivery, yet it does not state what play should look like.

The Early Education publication of *Development Matters in the Early Years Foundations Stage*, as a non-statutory guidance, hopes to support early child-hood practitioners in implementing the requirements of the EYFS, and attempts to break down play. Further, at the bottom of each page in the *Development Matters* guidance it clearly states that the development statements and their order should not be taken as necessary steps for individual children. They should not be used as checklists. Yet to achieve the statutory requirement of the early learning goals, 'providers must help children work towards (the knowl-edge, skills and understanding children should have at the end of the academic year in which they turn five)' (DfE, 2012, p. 2). This can be interpreted by early childhood practitioners in working through the development statements as a form of checklist to ensure children are on the right track to meeting the early learning goals.

Operational challenges and dilemmas impacting the EYFS

The most valuable resource as part of an 'enabling environment' to any early years setting is the early childhood practitioners themselves. Research illustrates the impact 'effective', 'knowledgeable' and 'competent skilled' practitioners have on children's learning and development (Moyles *et al.*, 2002; Sylva *et al.*, 2004; Urban *et al.*, 2011). Not having enough or having those with poor skills, qualities and knowledge leads to poor quality experiences for young children. Syeda's dilemma (see Vignette 2) is not unfamiliar to those in management roles, but sickness cannot be helped, and then there is the high staff turnover as a result of poor pay and status (Early Education, 2010, p. 18) which continues to haunt early years settings (Penn, 2000). However, the statutory framework for the EYFS is clear regarding ratios of children to adults.

Ratios are a legal requirement of the EYFS. This is the number of children allowed per adult within an early years setting, dependent on age. For example, the legal requirement for children aged under two must be one member of staff for every three children. Ratios challenge the demands of delivering the EYFS, as very often early years providers abide by the minimum requirement stipulated by the

Vignette 2

Reflective journal entry of a nursery manager's day in a nursery setting

Syeda is the nursery manager of a setting that caters for 50 children aged zero to five years. The nursery opens at 7am to allow staff enough time to set up before the children and their parents arrive at 8am. Syeda is due in a little later; however, at 8am she receives a call from the setting informing her that two staff members from the pre-school room have called in sick and therefore the setting is short staffed according to the expected ratios of the day.

Syeda gets to the setting and although she makes herself part of the ratios immediately, she calls her local recruitment agency for help. The two temporary workers who arrive, not familiar with the setting at all, take on supervisory roles throughout the day, where they watch and interact only when the children speak to them. Amy, who is a member of staff in the preschool room, had planned to conduct observations on her key children, but had to take on additional duties due to the absence of her colleagues and therefore could not do so. Claire had planned a visit with a group of children to the local hairdressers as a means of linking with the wider community, but had to cancel due to ratio issues.

EYFS and will not recruit extra practitioners. Syeda as the manager was able to keep to the minimum ratios with aid from the recruitment agency, which many settings cannot afford to do due to income restrictions. However, the real issues are being dealt with by the children and the remaining staff.

Evangelou *et al.* (2009, p. 23) describe children's learning and development as arising from the interplay between the 'interconnected and dynamic facets of the unique child with [their] surrounding relationships and experience'. This means that relationships and experiences influence children's learning and development, relationships and experiences that very often involve adults. From the moment children are born they are engaged in interacting with adults. Building on Bronfenbrenner's ecological model, where relationships and experiences are part of an interwoven web of influences on young children's learning and development, the ecological domains of the microsystem, mesosystem, exosystem and macrosystem are clearly represented in the EYFS. The framework positions the *unique child* at the centre by recognising that 'every child is a competent learner', with the interaction of positive relationships and enabling environments to support the child's learning and development as 'themes and principles' that are focused around the child (Development Matters, 2012). This demonstrates the powerful influence that relationships and experiences have on children and why the EYFS further builds on the ratio requirement to advocate the key person approach for practitioners. Yet the absence of these positive relationships in Syeda's setting for those children whose key person is not available tests children's experiences, the EYFS themes and the EYFS key person approach of placing the child at the centre of curriculum delivery.

The key person approach is intense, involving hard work and a significant professional and emotional commitment (DCSF, 2007, p. 1). Embedded in Bowlby and Ainsworth's theory of attachment, where attachment is the bond between carer and child, the EYFS advocates that a key person is available for each child, and that they develop a genuine bond and close relationships with children. A key person needs to demonstrate three characteristics: availability, sensitivity and warmth (Siren Film, 2007). For children in Syeda's setting whose key person is not 'available', their attachments are disrupted. Strangers in the form of agency workers who take on the role on a temporary basis need to be sensitive to these emotional attachments, but this is difficult as neither the setting nor the children are familiar to them. Bain and Barnett (cited in Elfer *et al.*, 2012, p. 23) use the term 'multiple indiscriminate care' to describe the care received by children through large, continuous, multiple changing adults rather than a specific key person. Palaiologou and Hallowes (2010) further describe this as 'vertical transitions' where children can move between various people and places throughout the day. In the day-to-day practicalities of the early years context it is difficult to keep the key person approach active. Unavoidable and unplanned situations where children's attachments are disrupted, tested by ratios, shift work, absences and long operational hours of work, leave no scope for a second key person for children when the main one is away. In reality, those key persons that are present actually are made 'unavailable' for their own key children in order to cover these operational challenges and dilemmas, mainly to deal with domestic activities, as demonstrated in Amy and Claire's case.

Adhering to minimum ratios impacts upon the time Amy has to fulfil the requirements of the EYFS, which include time to observe, assess and plan. She was not able to conduct her observations to then use her knowledgeable competence to inform further effective skilled learning experiences for her key children. This contradicts the EYFS, where it frames the role of the practitioner as crucial in observing and reflecting, planning and resourcing (Swarbrick, 2007, p. 118). Due to minimum ratios and lack of staff, Claire had to cancel her trip to the local community, which then hinders her group's learning and hence the EYFS in practice. Both practitioners had to keep the room operational through the practical tasks necessary to ensure the smooth running of the setting and the room. The community and relationships play a key role in promoting children's development, as demonstrated by Bronfenbrenner's model and the key person approach, yet operational challenges and dilemmas continue to test and hinder an effective curriculum for children through the limited 'availability' of effective, knowledgeable, competent and skilled practitioners to deliver a quality curriculum.

The learning environment and the EYFS

Brooker (2005) describes the practice in early years settings as embedded in 'ideological tradition', a view that the roots of practice in working with children have evolved historically from previous ideas, some of which have been held by individuals and some where particular practice has always 'worked'. The most influential of all ideas within this ideological tradition are those of the Swiss developmental psychologist Jean Piaget. The threads of Piagetian thinking are clearly embedded in the EYFS framework, and strangely in Colleen's practice

Vignette 3

Case study of a practitioner's experience in a children's centre

Colleen set up the continuous provision areas in the toddler room. The areas consist of the home corner, sand and water area, small world play, construction, book area, art, music and mark making. When the children return from outside, Colleen is designated to three areas: the home corner, sand and water, and mark making.

Two-and-a-half-year-old Shola is in the home corner and role playing a doctor. Using a funnel from the sand and water area, Shola places it on a teddy bear's chest and puts her ear to the funnel. Another child comes in and Shola tells her that she is 'listening to teddy, he is sick'. For a while she stands staring at the teddy. She then drops the funnel and goes over to the other child and plays with the dressing-up clothes.

Meanwhile, Colleen does not see any of this as she is engrossed in the sand and water area where she is telling two children to share.

(Vignette 3). Children's learning and development appear as seven separate areas in the EYFS; Piaget's developmental theory also advocates separate phases in children's learning and development. In practice, the environment of Colleen's setting echoes separate areas of provision, i.e. the sand and water area, book area, construction, etc. Yet strangely, physically observing children moving in and out of each area does not make apparent to the practitioners the holistic and interconnected nature of children's learning and development.

Piaget believed that children develop in a linear stage, sensorimotor stage, preoperational stage, concrete operational stage and formal operational stage. The EYFS supporting material, *Development Matters,* continues to echo this tradition by breaking the seven areas of learning and development into ages and stages which consist of what children are learning at a certain stage and early learning goals that are also related to age (Soler and Miller, 2003, p. 61). In Colleen's setting, the children are also grouped according to ages: the toddler room caters for two year olds only, who will progress into the next room when they reach the age of three.

The EYFS further goes on to promote the notion of an 'enabling environment' where the physical environment plays a key role in supporting and extending children. Piaget also emphasised the child as an active explorer who moves through the processes of 'assimilation' and 'accommodation' via the environment they come into contact with. The practitioner's emphasis on a resource-rich environment, and her focus on her role as a provider of all this, where Shola had ample opportunities to explore, echoes Piagetian theory. However, whether intentionally or unintentionally, the practitioner's absence from Shola's play demonstrates another thread of Piaget's thinking: adults ceasing to be a part of the learning once the environment has been prepared for the children.

In a busy setting, where ratios are strictly adhered to, practitioners often find themselves divided into a number of activity areas, and divided among the children they come into contact with. Here there is a concern regarding the amount of time practitioners are able to dedicate to the child-initiated learning that the EYFS advocates (Keating *et al.,* 2002, p. 198), as provision alone does not automatically promote learning and development (Sylva *et al.,* 2004, p. 111). This leads to practitioners taking on more of a supervisory role than an interactive, supporting one. Shola's abrupt pause in her self-initiated role play of a doctor demonstrates that she did not know what more to do with the sick teddy, hence her decision to go and play elsewhere. The practitioner's absence at this point did not move Shola on in her learning, or widen the areas of development in which she was engaged. A study by Hedges *et al.* (2011) into an interest-led curriculum in New Zealand advocates the notion of 'funds of knowledge', which emphasises the importance of existing knowledge which children bring into settings and into their play. This was clearly demonstrated in Shola's play where someone who was sick needed treatment from a doctor. This demonstrated a richness of prior knowledge which needed the practitioner's effective, knowledgeable and competent practice to further enhance and build on to take Shola forward. This clearly indicates that the provision of resources and opportunities for exploration must be accompanied by appropriate intervention from adults (Moyles and Adams, 2001).

Although the EYFS and the setting echo the 'ideological tradition' of Piaget, they also emphasise learning and development as a social activity. Embedded in the sociocultural perspective of learning and development of Lev Vygotsky (1978), the EYFS promotes the importance of the ways in which adults shape and support learning. It emphasises the need for interaction and dialogue between the child and the adult to further 'scaffold' learning and development. The EYFS clearly signposts the role of the practitioner in supporting children; however, the practical realities inhibit this approach. Shola needed a 'knowledgeable', 'competent' and 'skilled' adult's support to understand what she was doing and where she could go with their 'effective' support through her 'zone of proximal development' (Vygotsky, 1978). However, the layout of the learning environment and deployment of practitioners within this did not move Shola forward.

There is a strong emphasis on child-initiated activities in the EYFS, and on children selecting their own resources and making choices. The organisation of the

Vignette 4

Observation note of child-to-child interaction in a nursery setting

Noor, four, and Joshua, three, were building a house in the construction area. 'I want to fix my sky to the roof,' said Joshua. 'There's nothing to stick it with,' replied Noor. She paused and then went to the art area. She came back with some masking tape and together the two children fixed their satellite dish to their home.

'Shall we paint a picture to put in the house?' asked Noor. Joshua said it was a good idea and both children went to the paint area. However, they found no easel and the shelf which normally contained paint was broken. The easel in the art area had been broken for weeks now and, although a request had been made to management for a new one, the practitioners had not set up any other creative activities.

learning environment is important in facilitating child-initiated play. As the EYFS clearly states: 'Practitioners offer stimulating resources . . . rich learning opportunities' (Development Matters, 2012, p. 2).

The theme of the enabling environment establishes the understanding that for children to be successful in their learning and development they need access to a well-resourced and organised environment. This was evident in Noor and Joshua's play (Vignette 4), where the provision of some resources and space was organised to promote integrated learning experiences. The environment allowed Noor and Joshua to move into different areas to complete their construction and thus they were able to make a choice over how they would like to furnish their home and then go on to another area. Bruce (2001, p. 46) suggests that free-flow play is 'coordinated, moves fluidly from one phase or scenario to the next and makes young children feel powerful and contented'. This also demonstrates the importance of a well-resourced environment in order for this to take place. However, in our scenario, both children were disappointed when they could not find the resources they needed to complete the play they had initiated.

It is clear that the children had sufficient space, time and choice, with a range of activities. However, Vygotsky's (1978) notion of the 'zone of proximal develop-ment' was inhibited because the children needed to reach the height of their play with support from resources that were not available. Keating et al.'s (2002) research into reception teachers' responses to the curriculum found concerns regarding the availability of resources for children to select from to support their independent learning where resources were limited. For this setting, the reasons clearly seem to be related to supply and budgets. In order to implement the requirements of the EYFS, it is clear that money needs to be available. Some settings generate their income solely through charging parents fees for their children to attend the setting, of which staff costs account for the highest pro-portion. This then restricts the investment that settings can make in resourcing, equipping and maintaining an enabling environment for the child-initiated approach that the EYFS advocates, thus impacting yet again the effective imple-mentation of the EYFS curriculum in practice.

Beliefs, values, attitudes and the EYFS

The EYFS principle approach advocates that children should learn to be strong and independent, but within a base of loving, secure positive relationships. Further, the personal, social and emotional learning and development prime

Vignette 5

Parent induction feedback record in an early years settings

Three-year-old Carlos has just started at his local early years setting. On his second day, Carlos's father arrives to collect him. Before approaching the room Carlos is based in, his father can hear him. As he walks into the room, he can't see his son but manages to locate the sound coming from the toilet area. Outside is a staff member, sitting at a table completing some paperwork. When Carlos's father walks into the toilet area, he finds Carlos, who tells him that he was asking for help to wash his hands. Upon querying this with the staff member, her response was that 'he needs to be independent and the only way he can learn is to do things for himself'.

area of the EYFS guidance states that early childhood practitioners should support the development of independence skills, particularly for children who are highly dependent upon adult support for personal care, through 'offering support to children in new situations' (Development Matters, 2012, p. 11). Carlos's experience differs here (Vignette 5). It is obvious that the guidance clearly states that independence in young children has to be supported. The guidance further provides practice direction in what adults 'could do'. However, here the issue of personal beliefs, values and attitudes in how children should learn and develop take effect.

Beliefs, values and attitudes can be regarded as the system of thinking in one's practice. The early childhood practitioner has her own thinking on how children should learn to be independent – the notion 'you must learn for yourself' – which may clash with the setting's beliefs and values as well as those of the parents and those that determine the EYFS. Brock's (2006) research into the dimensions of early years professionalism emphasises that working with young children is not just about having qualifications, skills, knowledge, experience and meeting standards, but also about attitudes (ibid, p. 1). Attitudes, and to an extent the knowledge held by the practitioners as well as values and beliefs, will underpin how the EYFS is approached and implemented. *Key Elements of Effective Practice* (KEEP) (2005) defines six areas which are key to effective practice. The document highlights the need for an 'agreed view' on what constitutes an effective practitioner in order to effectively support children, and attitudes are highlighted as one of them:

The purpose of defining effective practice for early years practitioners is to set out the attitudes, knowledge, understanding and skills needed to put the Principles for Early Years Education into practice.

(KEEP, 2005, p. 6)

Here there is a conflict, as setting out knowledge, understanding and skills needed for effective practice can be tested and demonstrated. Interviews and induction processes in settings are tailored to assist in this, as well as in-house training and qualification frameworks. Learning outcomes that are embedded in continuous professional development courses and degree programmes set out the knowledge, understanding and skills that will be assessed to successfully complete the courses. However, attitudes are missing from this framework. The attitude of a practitioner may be caught between the direct interaction of the child and practitioner and their actual implementation of the curriculum, as demonstrated by Carlos's practitioner. This suggests that the curriculum cannot be predetermined – it is constructed on a daily basis in the interactions between the practitioner and the child and the contextual situations they find themselves in. However, one must also remember that sometimes approaches towards the implementation of the curriculum are not down to attitudes or beliefs and values but what actually 'works'. 'If it's worked for the past 15 years then it will work now!' Or sometimes a worry about what may be found at Ofsted inspections will make a practitioner work differently (Swarbrick, 2007, p. 110). In Carlos's scenario, the practitioner was engaged in paperwork, which could be the very reason why she approached the situation as she did. This in itself is a challenge, where practitioners have been working in the same way for years and find it difficult to change (Stacey, 2009, p. 8). In addition, the EYFS has still failed to address the need for time for practitioners to consolidate their paperwork.

It is also important to note that beliefs, values and attitudes can vary significantly between individual practitioners. A personal philosophy is unique, a practitioner's own views on children and families (Arthur *et al.*, 2008) that has been inherited through their personal and work histories (Stacey, 2009, p. 12). However, this can cause a conflict of values and approaches in what is determined as a quality curriculum for young children. As Moss and Pence (1994, p. 173) highlight, that quality to a large extent is determined by the 'eye of the beholder', in other words a quality curriculum is interpreted by early years practitioners rather than the EYFS. Arthur *et al.* (2008, p. 176) support this further by stating: 'What we value and believe to be important in early childhood education and in our work with children and families will largely determine our practices.' This is evident in Carlos's practitioner who believes that independence is a self-learned process and does not require the presence of another capable person.

It is apparent that implementing a curriculum which is effective for young children relies not only on knowledgeable and competent practitioners but hugely on the belief systems that govern each individual adult. Overcoming the issues of individual beliefs, values and attitudes is the largest challenge in the implementation of any curriculum, as practitioner effectiveness, knowledge and competence are underpinned by personal attitudes, beliefs and values (Sylva *et al.*, 2002, p. 104). What we believe about children affects how we relate to them. As early childhood practitioners, our beliefs, values and attitudes can enhance and determine the provision that we provide (Arthur *et al.*, 2008), but also affect the way we deliver the curriculum.

EYFS and time

The EYFS framework has to be 'interpreted', then 'transferred' and 'applied' in practice (Urban, 2008, p. 141). The most challenging aspect of this is the need for time. Challenges described in this chapter and many more in the complex work of early years practitioners highlight the concern for the amount of time needed in fulfilling the requirements of the EYFS, whether directly with the children or away from them. The EYFS stresses the importance of assessment in helping early childhood practitioners recognise children's progress, understand their needs and plan activities to support them (DfE, 2012, p. 10). In Keiran's case (Vignette 6), the requirements of this necessitate his time away from the children where he is able to analyse and assess his observations to inform an 'effective' plan. The EYFS further promotes the notion of the balance of adult-led and child-initiated play, informed by the study of Effective Provision of Pre-school Education (EPPE), where research suggests that child outcomes are better if this balance is achieved. Yet here Keiran overpowers the use of adult-led practice by determining the pace of children's learning. He needed to complete his assessment and planning as he was accountable to the manager, and therefore directed the children's play on his terms to achieve this. Here again, there could be the tension that exists in what the practitioner believes being in conflict with being 'accountable' and the need of 'evidence' in his procedures with children. The Tickell Review (2011) has recognised this need for time to interact with children through the reduction of paperwork. The new EYFS has responded by reducing the curriculum framework's content. However, what still has not been addressed by the EYFS is allocating time for practitioners to undertake assessment, but also time to review and consolidate their practices to enable a quality curriculum for children and to remain motivated through continuous professional development.

THE EARLY YEARS CURRICULUM

Vignette 6

Case study of a practitioner's experience in a nursery setting

Keiran is an early years practitioner in a privately run day nursery. The operational hours are 8am to 6pm. Keiran wants to get started on his planning for the following week and makes a start, but within ten minutes of analysing observations, he is called back into the room as another member of staff is due to take a break. Keiran is assigned to the construction area and while the children are playing he decides to continue with his planning as it is due in at the end of the day for the room supervisor to check. At this point he looks up frequently but does not interact with the children.

The children start running around with the constructions they have made. Keiran twice warns them to stop running, but the third time asks them to tidy up and go and sit in the book area for some quiet time. Later Keiran is reminded that there is a staff meeting in the evening starting at 6.30pm, providing that the last child has been collected by then.

Huberman (1995) defines the term 'open networks' where practitioners should remain open to insights from other practitioners, as well as children and parents, to develop their approaches with children, something that yet again needs time. Lave and Wenger's (1991) situated learning theory on developing 'communities of practice' requires practitioners with a common aim or passion to interact regularly with other practitioners, parents, multi-professional networks and, most importantly, the children. For Keiran, the 'open networks' and 'communities of practice' interaction seems to be in the evening after the nursery closes. Many settings cannot afford to close for half a morning to allow practitioners time to engage with their practices through reflection and development. Where settings run for long operational hours, staff are usually asked to stay back in the evening for meetings, often tired from a long day and unpaid. This then does not allow a conducive context for reflection and review for consolidation of practice to take place.

Reflection is the 'buzz' word that surrounds the early years. This entails the idea that quality effective implementation of a curriculum can be achieved through ongoing reflection by the competent practitioner. Donald Schon's (1991) work is highly regarded in influencing the way we think and approach reflective practice and the concept of the reflective practitioner. This is through 'reflection in action' where practitioners think on their feet while in interaction with the children, and 'reflection on action' where practitioners have time away to think after a situation. The SPEEL research further defines the qualities of an effective practitioner as one who engages in reflection and questioning. Further, Moss (2006, p. 36) terms the 'worker as a researcher' where practitioners reflect on their practice with the child in the centre of this reflection. This all indicates that reflection is expected of early childhood practitioners (Paige-Smith and Craft, 2008), yet time is needed for such reflection to take place.

The previous EYFS Principles into Practice cards all contained a section on 'reflecting on practice', which has now been removed. In the challenging and continually changing work contexts of practitioners, there is limited opportunity and time to step away and question 'What are we doing for children and how?' and 'Why do we do what we do?', to not only 'evaluate all aspects of effective pedagogy and child development' (Moyles *et al.*, 2002, p. 57) but 'plan to improve *curriculum* [my emphasis] practice or defend existing ones' (Swarbrick, 2007, p. 111). Urban (2008, p. 144) calls this 'reflective conversations' with the situations that practitioners find themselves in, by reframing the situation in order to both understand and change it. However, time is the essential component to allow such a conversation, and this is missing in the context of the EYFS. Time is needed to co-construct meaning alongside the children in order to understand their experiences to support and encourage learning (Paige-Smith and Craft 2008, p. 87). Nutbrown (2006) emphasises that unless early childhood practitioners come together to share and discuss practice – I argue, effective curriculum practice – practitioners' roles as advocates for children weaken as they are unable to articulate their views on what children need or to challenge policy and practice that do not place the child at the centre. This discussion of practice can also lead to critically engaging with policy implementation that does not take into account the inherent challenges, in this case within the EYFS, by the workforce.

Conclusion

The EYFS, with its many critiques, is undoubtedly a cornerstone in the history of early childhood in giving recognition to young children as having a clear, separate phase of learning and development, but also in its attempt at creating a universal curriculum. However, the EYFS also brings with it many challenges for early childhood practitioners that are visible only when engaging with the document and children in order to visualise what an effective quality curriculum looks like in practice. The curriculum is determined by the day-to-day work and interaction of early childhood practitioners with the children and the contexts they function in, which in many cases is difficult to capture in a document of practice guidelines. Practitioners bring with them their own ideals of what a curriculum should constitute, how children should learn and develop, and how they interpret the EYFS, which all filter down to test the function of the curriculum in practice. Operational challenges, the curriculum context and the limited time practitioners have all conflict with the EYFS as a framework and the EYFS in practice. Yet early childhood practitioners face this tension and conflict on a daily basis.

The reduced version of the EYFS seems to be a welcome change, but it has yet to be seen whether the 2012 EYFS allows early childhood practitioners to gain professional autonomy, creativity and flexibility in the use and implementation of the EYFS, or if it will continue to challenge the 'effective, knowledgeable, competent and skilled' early years practitioner in implementing an effective early years curriculum.

Reflective Questions

1. This chapter highlights some challenges in the implementation of the EYFS. Can you think of any further challenges or issues that may impact on curriculum delivery?

2. How has time constrained the implementation of an effective curriculum in your practice?

3. What are your beliefs, values and attitudes on how children learn and develop? How do these beliefs and values influence your practice?

References

Arthur, L., Beecher, B., Death, E., Dockett, S. and Farmer, S. (2008) *Programming and Planning in Early Childhood Settings* (4th Edition), Melbourne: Thomson.

Bain, A. and Barnett, L. (1986) 'The design of a day care system in a nursery setting for children under five: an abridged version of a report of an action research project', in Elfer, P., Goldschmied, E. and Selleck, D. (2012) *Key Persons in the Early Years: Building relationships for quality provision in early years settings and primary schools* (2nd Edition), Oxford: Routledge.

Brock, A. (2006) 'Dimensions of early years professionalism: attitudes versus compe-
tences?' *Reflecting on Early Years Issues, Training, Advancement and Co-operation in
Teaching Young Children*. Available online at: www.tactyc.org.uk/reflections_
papers.asp.

Brooker, L. (2005) 'Learning to be a child: cultural diversity and early years ideology', in
Yelland, N. (ed.) *Critical Issues in Early Childhood Education*, Maidenhead: Open
University Press.

Bruce, T. (2001) *Learning through Play, Babies, Toddlers and the Foundation Years*,
London: Hodder & Stoughton.

Craft, A. and Paige-Smith, A. (2008) 'Reflective practice', in Miller, L. and Cable, C (eds.)
Professionalism in the Early Years, London: Hodder.

David, T. (2004) 'Questions of quality: the contribution of research evidence to definitions of quality in early childhood education and care practice', in Schonfeld, H.,
O'Brien, S. and Walsh, T. (eds.) *Questions of Quality: Proceedings of a conference on
defining, assessing and supporting quality in early childhood care and education*, Dublin:
Centre for Early Childhood Development and Education.

Department for Children, Schools and Families (DCSF) (2004) *Every Child Matters:
Change for children*, Nottingham: DfES.

Department for Children, Schools and Families (DCSF) (2007) *Effective Practice:
KeyPerson approach*, Nottingham: DCSF.

Department for Children, Schools and Families (DCSF) (2008) *The Early Years
Foundation Stage: Setting the standards for learning, development and care for children
from birth to five*, DCSF Publications.

Department for Education (DfE) (2011) *Reforming the Early Years Foundation Stage
(EYFS): Government response to consultation*, DfE. Available online at: www.education.
gov.uk/consultations/downloadableDocs/Government%20response%20doc%
20191211%201630%20finaltext%20KM%20CB%201808(v2).pdf.

Department for Education (DfE) (2012) *Statutory Framework for the Early Years
Foundation Stage: Setting the standards for learning, development and care for children
from birth to five*, DfE.

Development Matters (2012) *Development Matters in the Early Years Foundation Stage
(EYFS)* London: Early Education/The British Association for Early Childhood
Education.

Early Education (2010) *Early Education Response to the Tickell Review of the Early Years
Foundation Stage: Call for evidence*, London: Early Education.

Evangelou, M., Sylva, K., Kyriacou, M., Wild, M. and Glenny, G. (2009) *Early Years
Learning and Development Literature Review*, London: DCSF.

Hedges, H., Cullen, J. and Jordan, B. (2011) 'Early years curriculum: funds of knowledge
as a conceptual framework for children's interests', *Journal of Curriculum Studies*,
43(2), 185–205.

Horvath, M. (2011) *Play and Exploration, Early Years Foundation Stage Forum*. Available online at: http://eyfs.info/articles/articleprinter.php?127.

Huberman, M. (1995) 'Networks that alter teaching: conceptualisations, exchanges and experiments', in *Teacher and Teaching: Theory and Practice*, 1(2), 193–211.

Keating, I., Basford, J., Hodson, E. and Harnett, A. (2002) 'Reception teacher responses to the Foundation Stage', *International Journal of Early Years Education*, 10(3), 193–203.

KEEP (2005) *Key Elements of Effective Practice*, Department for Education and Skills. Available online at: www.niched.org/resources.html.

Lave, J. and Wenger, E. (1991) *Situated Learning: Legitimate peripheral participation*, University Press.

Moss, P. (2006) 'Structures, understandings and discourses: possibilities for re-envisioning the early childhood worker', *Contemporary Issues in Early Childhood*, 7(1), 30–41. Available online at: http://dx.doi.org/10.2304/ciec.2006.7.1.30.

Moss, P. and Pence, A. (1994) *Valuing Quality in Early Childhood Services: New approaches to defining quality*, London: Chapman.

Moyles, J. and Adams, S. (2001) *StEPs: Statements of Entitlement to Play*, Buckingham: Open University Press.

Moyles, J., Adams, S. and Musgrove, A. (2002) *SPEEL Study of Pedagogical Effectiveness in Early Learning*, Department for Education and Skills (DfES) Research Report 363, Norwich: HMSO.

Musgrave, J. (2010) 'Educating the future educators: the quest for professionalism in early childhood education', in *Contemporary Issues in Early Childhood*, 11(4), 435–442.

Nutbrown, C. (2006) *Threads of Thinking: Young children learning and the role of early education* (3rd Edition), London: Sage.

Oberhuemer, P. (2005) 'Conceptualising the early childhood pedagogue: policy approaches and issues of professionalism', *European Early Childhood Education Research Journal*, 13(1), 5–16.

Palaiologou, I. and Hallowes A. (2010) 'Effective transitions into and out of the Early Years Foundation Stage to Key Stage 1', in Palaiologou, I. (ed.) *Early Years Foundation Stage: Theory and practice*, London: SAGE.

Penn, H. (2000) *Early Childhood Services*, Buckingham: Open University Press.

Schon, D. A. (1991) *The Reflective Turn: Case studies in and on educational practice*, New York: Teachers Press.

Siren Film (2007) *Life at Two*, DVD and transcript, Newcastle: Siren Film and Video Ltd.

Soler, J. and Miller, L. (2003) 'The struggle for early childhood curricula: a comparison of the English Foundation Stage Curriculum, Te Whariki and Reggio Emilia', *International Journal of Early Years Education*, 11(1), 57–67.

Stacey, M. (2009) *Teamwork and Collaboration in Early Years Settings*, Exeter: Learning Matters.

Swarbrick, N. (2007) 'Formal and informal curricula', in Mitchell, H. and Wild, M. (eds.) *Early Childhood Studies: A reflective reader*, Exeter: Learning Matters.

Sylva, K., Melhuish, E., Sammons, P., Siraj-Blatchford, I. and Taggart, B. (2004) *The Effective Provision of Pre-school Education [EPPE] Project Final Report*, London: Department for Education and Skills. Available online at: http://publications. education.gov.uk/eOrderingDownload/SSU-FR-2004-01.pdf.

Tickell, D. C. (2011) *The Early Years: Foundations for life, health and learning*. An independent report on the Early Years Foundation Stage to her Majesty's Government. Available online at: www.education.gov.uk/tickellreview.

Tovey, H. (2007) *Playing Outdoors: Spaces and places, risks and challenges*, Buckingham: Open University Press.

Urban, M. (2008) 'Dealing with uncertainty: challenges and possibilities for the early childhood profession', *European Early Childhood Education Research Journal*, 16(2), 135–152.

Urban, M., Vandenbroeck, M., Peeters, J., Lazzari, A. and Van Laere, K. (2011) *CoRe. Competence Requirements in Early Childhood Education and Care*. Research documents commissioned by the European Commission, DG Education and Culture. Available online at: http://ec.europa.eu/education/more-information/doc/2011/core_en.pdf.

Vygotsky, L. (1978) *Mind in Society: The development of higher psychological processes*, London: Harvard University Press.

Watkins, C. and Mortimer, P. (1999) 'Pedagogy: what do we know?', in Mortimer, P. (ed.) *Understanding Pedagogy and its Impact on Learning*, London: Paul Chapman Publishing.

4

Providing an inclusive early years curriculum through physical learning

Carrie Weston

Overview

This chapter considers the centrality of movement, physical learning and activity within early years educational practice. Evidence is explored to support the view that young children learn *through* and *with* the physical. It will be argued that understanding the young child as an embodied learner allows for both unique and universal configurations of childhood; in other words, that it is a holistic, inclusive concept. Through considering potential barriers to physical learning in the early years curriculum, this chapter raises questions about pedagogical approaches and physical learning within a truly inclusive early years curriculum.

Key Themes

- Young children as active and physical learners.
- Movement experiences in early learning.
- The embodiment of cognition.

Introduction

It is recognised in both theory and practice that physical and intellectual development are closely interwoven in early childhood. The journey from birth to maturity is a period of rapid development for both the mind and the body, none more so than in the early years of life. It takes little more than casual observation to witness that babies and young children use their body parts, physical movements and senses to explore surroundings and objects, to form relationships, to express emotions and to seek both pleasure and comfort. From the moment of birth, it is through movement and the physical self that children begin to 'engage with the world, supporting all their learning, through movement and physical sensations' (HMSO, 2011, p. 94). This chapter considers that an understanding of the child as an embodied learner leads, necessarily, to a holistic and inclusive pedagogical approach. In other words, it is important to offer young learners opportunities to develop and express knowledge and competencies beyond the boundaries of traditional measures of logic and linguistic ability. It is in this sense that embodiment is an inclusive concept, widening the scope for the development of learning and assessment for young children. We will look at how the capacity for learning through physical means can be maximised within the early years curriculum.

In England, the 2011 review of the Early Years Foundation Stage (EYFS), concerning the education and welfare of children from zero to five years, placed increased emphasis on physical development as a prime area of the EYFS. In doing so, the importance of movement and physical activity in early childhood is recognised as essential in the personal, social and emotional development of the child. As children develop motility and mastery of their body, so they experience themselves as active agents within their world. This, in turn, promotes 'growth in confidence and awareness of control; it supports communication and language because a child who can effectively use large movements, gestures and the fine movements involved in speech is able to convey messages to others' (HMSO, 2011, p. 95). This renewed emphasis on physical development is to be lauded, while at the same time offering the chance for scrutiny of practice within the early years curriculum. We need to ask ourselves just how often the child is considered as a *physical* learner within planning and assessment. In particular, when young children enter schooling, to what extent are physicality and action within learning experiences evident amid the more structured formality of the school setting?

In the early years, the body is the primary means of learning (Jennings, 1990). Indeed, it may be argued that it is only through senses, actions and interactions that understanding and reality are created (Gill, 2000). Babies and young children receive information through touch, movement and physical senses; concepts are developed through schema, as children move and interact with space and objects around them. It is widely considered that children develop physical abilities in a predictable order, something which is recognisable in teaching and learning which reflects 'age and stage' theories of child development. Most notably, Jean Piaget's still influential theory explains how young children construct knowledge through their physical actions and activity (Piaget, 1953). It is through physically 'doing' that young children experience and thus assimilate an understanding of the world around them. In Piagetian theory, physical interaction with objects and people will enable the child to construct mental representations and thereby start to hold understanding beyond the immediate and physical. This capacity to construct mental representations can grow only from concrete, physical experiences and facilitates the development of cognition, eventually allowing abstract thought. Early learning, therefore, is achieved by action and bodily experiences derived from physical activity (Athey, 1990). It makes sense that the young learner must be considered as *embodied*. Therefore, the greater the physical experiences and motile capacity of the child, the more opportunities for learning are created. In turn, this raises the question of what practitioners can do to maximise the physical learning potential of the child.

Barriers to physical learning

First it is perhaps pertinent to consider why such a question needs to be asked at all. While the notion of cognition as rooted in activity permeates much of the early years curriculum (e.g. High/Scope, EYFS), there are two potential barriers to understanding the child as embodied and a 'physical learner' which need examination.

To start with, constructivist understandings of child development (such as Piaget and Erikson, in the purest sense, but also Vygotsky and Bruner) assume a staged progression in the acquisition of knowledge, leading to a curriculum that is justified on the grounds of developmentally appropriate practice (DAP). The danger in assuming that child development is governed by general and universal factors is that practice considered appropriate to the understood stage of development becomes accepted practice. Yelland and Kilderry (2005) suggest that this carries with it a bias towards western society values and norms. While DAP has a tendency to rely on modernist, scientific-based theories about childhood, Corrie (1995) notes that practices resulting from such theories assume a shared and universal understanding of young children. This overlooks the value and significance of difference. Such an omission has implications for children from a variety of cultural and ethnic backgrounds and it also places many children with special educational needs and disabilities (SEND) at a disadvantage from the outset. How we understand the environment and world around us is very much dependent on our experiences of it through our physicality. Therefore, varying experiences of 'being' and 'doing' will naturally lead to many manifestations of understanding the environment, space, objects and others around us. These different understandings are rooted in the physical experiences and opportunities we have had, rather than in a predetermined notion of child development.

It is noted in the Tickell review of the EYFS (HMSO, 2011, p. 95) that it is through physical play and activity that children discover and practise skills of coordination, control, manipulation and movement. However, it is also noted that this is a 'process which may be restricted in childrearing practices using equipment to support and restrain babies and young children'. Similarly, the process may be restricted by opportunity, space, traditional or cultural practices, or by the specific needs of the individual. Thus, the theory of embodiment seems particularly relevant from a developmental perspective (Needham and Libertus, 2011). A contemporary understanding of the early years curriculum needs to unite established theories of linear child development with a postmodernist interrogation of assumptions in practice (Yelland and Killderry, 2005, p. 247). It is in the early years that the most dramatic changes in motor abilities occur, offering the potential for practitioners to foster learning through understanding the child in relation to physical experiences rather than physical development.

The second challenge to embodied, physical learning comes from the curriculum itself. As noted by Penn (2011, p. 127), emphasis is primarily on cognitive attributes, with 'the brain as the central organ'. This emphasis denies other potentialities and establishes traditional intellectual achievement above all else (Gardner, 1983). In a review of research, David (2003) notes that once young children enter compulsory schooling there is a growing emphasis on teaching content and a move towards specific subject areas, formality and whole-class teaching. While the 2011 Tickell review recognises the disconnect between the EYFS and Key Stage 1 of the English National Curriculum, there is hesitation in recommending greater emphasis on physical play and child-led learning when the child first enters school, as this does not reflect practices within the National Curriculum and traditional formal schooling. Once in school, young children are subject to testing and measuring of learning. The pressure for such measurable performance narrows the classroom experience (Ball, 1999) and requires teachers to produce evidence of learning in order that assessment criteria can be applied. All of these factors contribute towards a tendency to understand 'learning' as a sedentary, teacher-led activity with tangible, recordable learning outcomes. They militate against learning which places the child as the physical constructor of their own experiences and understanding.

Since 1979, control over what is taught and how has increasingly moved into the hands of ministers, driven by top-down pressures for measurable indicators (Anning, 1997) so that learning is structured towards what can be assessed and monitored. In other words, we want children to show that they know the things which are prescribed in the curriculum. Such outcomes, with a purely cognitive perspective, fail to consider the role of the body for assessing the child's true cognitive ability. Accordingly, the body is not considered as the primary means for learning. Indeed, in some instances (particularly in children with SEND) it becomes a roadblock that prevents a child's true competence from being revealed in their performance (Needham and Libertus, 2011). An emphasis on the cognitive leaves the young child disembodied, as educators focus on assessing logic and linguistic abilities which are not expressed through physicality.

Physical learning and transition to school

It is upon entering the phase of change between preschool and compulsory schooling that the understanding of the young child as an embodied learner becomes most challenged. The distinction between the intellectual and the physical can be seen to have roots in philosophical tradition, for example John Locke's *tabula rasa,* which established the 'blank' mind of the child to be meaningfully filled through education, or Descartes' (1641) separation of the mind and body as essentially different entities. Such understandings of learning place the development of intellect and ability firmly within the mind as a place distinct from the body. Indeed, the separation of mind and body was also held by Plato in the earliest description of the place and purpose of education (Republic, c.360 BC). This makes an interesting contrast with the quotation from François Rabelais (1494–1553), within the Tickell review (HMSO, 2011), that 'a child is not a vase to be filled, but a candle to be lit'.

Yet the dualistic (mind/body) view of the learner remains steadfast. Why is it that school physical education takes place within a separate and identified curriculum area, frequently in a different location, often demanding different clothing and sometimes even a different teacher? This certainly suggests that cognitive and physical learning are considered as separate and different. But an embodied view of learning would incorporate multiple and interacting factors, including cognition, physicality, context, culture and prior experiences. Seen from this perspective, Needham and Libertus (2011, p. 118) argue, the child's overt physical behaviour becomes extremely interesting, as it is multiply determined and offers the only concrete information allowing us to assess the child's ability. But how often do we use the child's physical behaviour as a measure in assessment?

Prior to school entry, many young children will have encountered one, or some, of a range of preschool experiences, from childminders to private nurseries, local authority day centres to parental home care. Despite the English EYFS, it is only at the age of school entry that compulsory attendance brings about some form of cohesion and unity in terms of geographical location and the standard of training for teachers. Debate surrounds the issue of whether compulsory school attendance at the age of four or five years is necessarily beneficial, and it is recognised that young children in the UK are introduced to a more formalised context at an earlier age than in many other European countries (Oliver *et al.*, 1998; Prais, 1997; Woodhead, 1989).

Still, it is only upon starting school that all children access a universal curriculum, learning environment and qualified teachers. Prior to that, the patchwork of preschool possibilities should serve to remind us that children do not enter the classroom with universal or equitable experiences. This is important when we remember the significance of sensory and physical experiences in children's learning development. Research on the relationship between physical movement and cognition (Ratey, 2008) suggests that learning and remembering are directly influenced by the physical movement a child has experienced. The opportunity for such movement will be influenced by the child's preschool experiences, environment, culture, socio-economic factors and dis/ability. It will be a complex inter-relationship between environmental, social and physical factors. So, to truly embrace Plowden's (1967, p. 1) recognised opening statement that 'at the heart of the educational process lies the child', it is therefore necessary to focus on the physical and embodied experiences that comprise the development of the child.

The embodied learner in the curriculum

Generally, we do not teach children to reach out, grab, crawl, walk, run and jump. It is assumed that these things just happen, that children develop motile capacities as part of their natural growth and maturation. Yet to avoid assumption, we must also accept that there are many factors influencing physical development and capabilities. By considering the child as the embodiment of these influential factors, practitioners can both confront and embrace the differences which children bring to their learning. This is at the heart of inclusion.

Seeing the child as embodied is to embrace differences between children, as, by definition, individuality is at the very centre of the existential experience. Conversely, differences are also negated by embodiment. If early education offers children the space and opportunity to physically explore, move and learn through interaction, then body and movement experiences are enhanced for all; differences in active experience will be reduced. For example, evidence suggests that children with learning disabilities struggle with crossing the midline of their own body (i.e. gross and fine right-to-left or up-and-down cross-body movement), which impacts on reading and writing skills within the traditional classroom setting (Pica, 2006). Considering the child as an embodied learner, the practitioner would provide physical and movement experiences which enhance learning. Experience of cross-lateral movement influences the conjunctive use of the right and left hemispheres of the brain, which is necessary in reading, writing and problem solving. This, then, gives us two strands within understanding the child as an embodied learner. First, it is necessary to offer the opportunity for 'kinaesthetic' learning, achieved through hands-on, practical experience such as touching, feeling and doing (see Gardner's 1983 'multiple intelligences' and Kolb's 1984 Experiential Learning Theory). Then, it is equally necessary to ensure that children gain mastery of their own body, understand how the different parts move and feel, explore how much force or resistance is required at the right time, and know how to physically relate to and interact with others in both defined and open spaces. Young children need opportunities to learn both through the physical and teaching, which allows the development of their physical knowledge and skills. In other words, to enable experience of bodily movements necessary to engage in kinaesthetic learning, the spatial awareness to enhance mathematical and logical thought, the fine motor skills necessary in writing, or the ability to express creativity and emotion non-dependent on linguistic ability, it is essential to provide specific teaching and learning opportunities which focus on physical movement and development in their own right.

Having argued for the importance of physical learning, the remainder of this chapter will focus on the teaching and learning of movement so that opportunities for physical experiences and body knowledge to facilitate active, physical learning and assessment are considered. Of course, it is not possible within the constraints of a chapter to fully explore movement teaching. Rather, it is the aim to examine and interrogate the purpose and possibilities of physical education within the curriculum for young learners.

Over the hurdles: developing embodiment through PE

As the young child moves between the preschool and compulsory phase of education, the curriculum naturally (although, conversely, artificially) places learning within categories. Physical education (PE) remains a compulsory subject, and while there is no intention to suggest here that physical learning should be restricted to a curriculum area, PE offers the opportunity to enhance the physical and motile capacities of children for use throughout their learning. As such, PE for young children is a fertile area.

Kirk (2006) identifies a paucity of research concerning PE in the early years, which is perhaps surprising given that early childhood is a time of rapid physical and intellectual growth; children learn *with* and *through* as well as *about* the physical. Furthermore, evidence suggests that many practitioners lack confidence in teaching PE (Ofsted, 2004; Weston, 2008) and while there is much emphasis on activity, there is often little purpose, intention or relationship to other curriculum areas. Yet, through developing motile capabilities within PE, children's potential to learn through embodiment and physical interaction is enhanced. Seen this way, PE becomes an invaluable opportunity to develop the learning experiences of young children, which can then be utilised in all areas within an interconnected and seamless early years curriculum.

The concept of physical education is nebulous. Former Prime Minister Gordon Brown's statement that 'you can't beat the joy of participating in sport . . . the thing I remember most about school was sport' (Kelso, 2008) will resonate with some people, while others may find Myerson's (2005, p. 51) description more befitting: 'Who wants, after all, on a chilly black autumn morning, to undress down to vest and pants and sit shuddering and goose-pimpled on a cold gym floor?' Neither view should, of course, be descriptive of young children's experiences of PE. However, such polarised views offer a starting point for examining embodiment within the only curriculum area with specific focus on the body.

Haydn-Davies (2005) suggests that the curriculum is heavily weighted with an emphasis on games and school sports, a point supported by Kirk (2004), who notes the increasing dominance of sport within PE. In England, the Physical Education, School Sport and Club Links strategy (DfES/DCMS, 2002) established specific time allocation for PE for all 5–16 year olds and encouraged a coaching approach to skill development. The addition of 'sport' and school games to early schooling is problematic, as it necessarily brings with it the imposition of adult-defined rules, tactics and outcomes. A focus on sport and games places the child as a receiver, rather than a constructor, of predetermined skills, knowledge and understanding, which, in the early years, misses the whole point about children learning physically.

Arguably, this manifestation of PE has come about through 'crisis discourses' concerning the health and fitness of children, leading us back to the dualistic view of mind and body discussed earlier. Issues such as childhood obesity, increased levels of type 2 diabetes and inactivity caused by time spent on computers and electronic games have current public, media and thus political attention. Additionally, the London 2012 Olympic Games and the omnipresent desire for national success in world sports have, it can be argued, served to separate 'body' from 'mind' in the way that physical education is conceptualised and positioned. Rather than an integral aspect of holistic development and a medium for learning, the PE curriculum is charged with the improvement of health and fitness and the nurturing of talent in specific, allocated and measured time. Treating PE as synonymous with sport reduces it to a narrow focus on discreet skills, with the added danger that the curriculum becomes merely a vehicle for addressing wider social issues. This is to ignore the diversity and complexity of childhood experiences and to inscribe the physical body with social value and meaning (Evans, 2004). There is a danger of understanding PE as a form of compensatory education with an end product deeply embedded in a modern and culturally influenced view of the 'healthy child'.

Rather, young children need to create knowledge and understanding in PE if it is to have authenticity. It needs to be embedded in their lived experiences, reflecting their social and cultural identity, in order for it to have purpose. For children with SEND, PE and movement are often problematised. Far from an inclusive concept, a focus on skill acquisition and team games leaves many children excluded from participation and achievement (Smith, 2004). What PE does offer, however, is the opportunity for specific time and space beyond the constraints of the classroom environment in which to explore and extend the range of physical competencies and bodily knowledge of the individual.

Davies (2003) suggests that individual movement is the starting point for PE in the early years. Emphasising developing movement experiences has a multi-faceted role in the lives of young children, as not only is movement central to the doing, thinking and feeling of children, it is part of the pleasure and sense of wellbeing experienced as they become able to maximise their bodily potential. Movement also plays a significant part in the development of thought, feeling and socialisation. Borrowing from the theories of Rudolf Laban (in Preston-Dunlop, 1998), movement facilitates physical experience of dynamics, space and relationships, learning through non-verbal communication and ergonomics. Experience and mastery of body movement, particularly within a group context, enables the development of thought, understanding and socialisation. This is also the fundamental principle of Sherborne Developmental Movement (SDM*), a programme of PE used frequently, although by no means exclusively, in 'special' schools, particularly with children with Autistic Spectrum Disorders (ASD). SDM is concerned with the capacity of the individual to develop relationships and build physical experiences through movement. The primary concern is not with the end product of movement but with the experiences of the child during the activity. Veronica Sherborne (2001, foreword, p. x) wrote: 'There is no element of competition in the movement experiences.' Developmental movement teaching aims to enable all children to feel 'at home' within their own bodies and to gain mastery of their movement in order to meet most effectively the challenges of the world around them. Through this self-mastery of the body, children develop their sense of identity in relation to the world and others, experiencing themselves as social, creative, moving individuals (Hill, 2006). SDM can provide the child with early experiences of success and confidence within a physical context (Dibbo and Gerry, 1995). Research-based evidence (Dibbo and Gerry, 1995; Hill, 2006; Marsden and Eggerton, 2007) supports Sherborne's work with young children by demonstrating that developmental movement teaching promotes the body knowledge, physical and emotional security, and self-confidence of all children, individually.

The value of movement and physical learning is also identified by Carpenter (2003). By giving credence to Howard Gardner's (1994) view of multiple intelligences, Carpenter suggests that bodily kinaesthetic intelligence should be valued in its own right. This would raise the status and value of PE within the curriculum, identifying it as the place for teachers to enable children to develop the necessary body knowledge to use in their active learning.

Particularly in the early years, the potential to utilise kinaesthetic learning is vast and appropriate to the interconnected curriculum where learning is predominantly experienced through the motor domain. Therefore, 'learning to move' becomes essential to the intellectual progress and affective development of young children. PE offers the opportunity to extend the movement vocabulary of children, in much the same way as practitioners recognise the necessity of building a child's experience of words through embedding them in meaning, purpose and sound in order to facilitate the process of reading and writing.

* For information on the Sherborne Association and courses on SDM, email: contact@sherbornemovementuk.org

The concept of physical literacy

The concept of physical literacy contrasts a Cartesian, dualist view, where the body merely houses the mind, with an existentialist, monistic view in which existence is embodied (Whitehead, 2001a, 2001b, 2004). Contemporary physical education, Whitehead (2001b, p. 6) argues, perpetuates the 'body-as-object' conceptualisation of the physical, demonstrated in debates about how much exercise is good for children and what food they eat. The concept of physical literacy in PE repositions the child as a whole, embodied being. Motile capacities are critical and the curriculum becomes less concerned with narrowly defined activities and outcomes and more concerned with the child's physical confidence and movement experiences. PE for young children should focus on body knowledge of balance, coordination, control, precise movement, strength, force and the ability to move at different speeds. Maude (2001) likens Whitehead's concept of physical literacy to Howard Gardner's 'bodily kinaesthetic intelligence' (cited in Haydn-Davies, 2005, p. 4). In other words, developing the physical literacy of children is to enhance their personal capabilities to know, explore and express through their bodies.

The focus of movement teaching is to enable children to develop motor skills and apply these to various contexts in order to develop understanding of the physical self in space, time and direction. The outcome, according to Whitehead (2006, p. 7), 'plays a very significant part in the development of self-realisation, self-confidence and positive self-esteem'. By enhancing in young children a fundamental range of basic motor skills, physical self-knowledge and bodily confidence, the child is able to engage holistically with the environment, opening up possibilities, opportunities and interaction experienced through their entire being. This 'presents a convincing argument for a shift in thinking which would help to empower primary teachers to understand and develop a rationale, and liberate them from the tyranny of thinking that they must know everything about sport before they can begin to teach physical education' (Talbot, 2005, p. 41).

Summary

If we accept that there is an inextricable link between physical and cognitive development, then the importance of maximising motile potential through providing opportunities for physical, embodied learning becomes apparent. In order to capitalise on the body and movement for learning, children first need to know and experience their bodies, their physical capabilities and their embodied self in relation to their environment, objects and other beings.

Physical learning is an integral part of the early years classroom, where children engage in activities designed to enhance understanding and develop knowledge – think of the young child manipulating coloured cubes in their counting, rolling and squashing plasticine, or active role playing in the home corner. This is embodied learning, where young children use their whole selves to engage in active learning experiences. It is through movement that children develop their understanding and express themselves – movement is the interconnection of communication, mental and physical activity.

This chapter has explored how PE is the only area of the curriculum specifically concerned with the development of the physical, and it is essential that the purpose therefore is to maximise the child's experience and knowledge of physical movement within their world. An understanding of the self as a physical, motile being in a social, interactive world is to have 'physical literacy' and a basis for all movement, learning and activity to come. This is not to deny children the right to learn specific physical skills to participate in games and sport for pleasure and health, but to provide a better, wider, more inclusive foundation from which to do so. Liberation from the experience of body-as-an-object is to enable children to feel comfortable within their own bodies, confident in what they can do, and embodied in their learning and daily lives.

It makes intuitive sense that children who are physically literate and comfortable with physical and social interaction will learn with and through each other more effectively. Movement teaching in the early years offers the potential to place the child, and not the curriculum, at the heart of learning. In order to both support and capitalise on the active, explorative, embodied learning of young children, we must first enable them to be physically literate.

Reflective Questions

1. In what ways do Piaget's theories suggest that the child is a physical learner?

2. How are inequalities in experiences likely to impact on a young child's understanding of the world?

3. How can practitioners develop the physical capabilities of children in order to maximise explorative, interactive learning?

4. Can you think of ways in which physical learning can be used within assessment in the early years?

References

Anning, A. (1997) *The First Years at School* (2nd Edition), Buckingham: Open University Press.

Athey, C. (1990) *Extending Thought in Young Children*, London: Paul Chapman.

Corrie, L. (1995) 'Vertical integration: teachers' knowledge and teachers' voice', *Australian Journal of Early Childhood*, 20(3), 1–5.

Ball, S. J. (1999) *Educational Reform and the Struggle for the Soul of the Teacher!* Faculty of Education, Hong Kong Institute of Educational Research, Chinese University of Hong Kong.

Carpenter, C. (2003) 'Factors affecting motor development', in Alfrey, C. (ed.) *Understand Children's Learning: A text for teaching assistants*, London: David Fulton, pp. 39–61.

David, T. (2003) *What Do We Know About Teaching Young Children?* Professional User Review based on BERA Academic Review, Canterbury: Christ Church University College.

Davies, M. (2003) *Movement and Dance in Early Childhood*, London: Paul Chapman.

Department for Education and Skills (DfES) and Department for Culture, Media and Sport (DCMS) (2002) *PE, School Sport and Club Links Strategy*, Nottingham: DfES Publications.

Dibbo, J. and Gerry, S. (1995) 'Physical education: Meeting the needs of the whole child', *British Journal of Physical Education*, Spring, 26(1).

Evans, J. (2004) 'Making a difference? Education and "ability" in physical education', *European Physical Education Review*, 10(1), 95–108.

Gardner, H. (1983) *Frames of Mind: The theory of multiple intelligences*, New York: Basic Books.

Gardner, H. (1993) *Multiple Intelligences*, New York: Basic Books.

Gill, J. (2000) *The Tacit Mode: Michael Polanyi's Postmodern Philosophy*, Albany, NY: State University of New York.

Haydn-Davies, D. (2005) 'How does the concept of physical literacy relate to what is and what could be the practice of physical education?', *British Journal of Teaching Physical Education*, 36(3), 43–48.

Hill, C. (2006) *Communicating Through Movement: Sherborne Developmental Movement towards a broadening perspective*, Stourbridge: Sunfield Publications.

HMSO (2011) *The Early Years: Foundations for life, health and learning.* An Independent Report on the Early Years Foundation Stage to Her Majesty's Government, Dame Clare Tickell.

Jennings, S. (1990) *Dramatherapy with Families, Groups and Individuals*, London: Jessica Kingsley.

Kelso, P. (2008) 'Brown backs the spirit of competition with £775m', *Guardian*, 2 February. Available online at: www.guardian.co.uk/politics/2008/feb/02/uk.london

Kirk, D. (2006) 'The "obesity crisis" and school physical education', *Sport, Education and Society*, 11(2), 121–133.

Kirk, D. (2004) 'Framing quality physical education: the elite sport model or sport education?', *Physical Education and Sport Pedagogy*, 9(2), 185–195.

Kolb, D. (1984) *Experimental Learning: Experience as the source of learning and development*, Englewood Cliffs, NJ: Prentice Hall.

Marsden, E. and Eggerton, J. (2007) *Moving with Research: Evidence-based practice in Sherborne Developmental Movement*, Clent: Sunfield Publications.

Maude, P. (2001) *Physical Children, Active Teaching*, Buckingham: Open University Press.

Myerson, J. (2005) *Not a Games Person*, London: Yellow Jersey Press.

Needham, A. and Libertus, K. (2011) 'Human intelligence is situated in a physical body and context: embodiment in early development', *Wiley Interdisciplinary Reviews: Cognitive Science*, 2(1).

Office for Standards in Education (2004) *Physical Education in Maintained Primary and Secondary Schools in England*, Ofsted, July.

Oliver, C., Smith, M. and Barker, S. (1998) 'Effectiveness of early interventions', *Treasury Supporting Papers for the Cross Departmental Review of Provision for Young Children*, London: HM Treasury.

Penn, H. (2011) *Quality in Early Childhood Services: An international perspective*, Berkshire: Open University Press.

Piaget, J. (1953) *The Origin of Intelligence in the Child*, London: Routledge and Keegan Paul.

Pica, R. (2006) *A Running Start: How play, physical activity and free time create a successful child*, New York: Marlowe & Co.

Plowden Report (1967) *Children and their Primary Schools*, London: HMSO.

Prais, S. J. (1997) *School-Readiness, Whole-Class Teaching and Pupils' Mathematical Attainments (Discussion Paper No.111)*, London: National Institute of Economic and Social Research.

Preston-Dunlop, V. (1998) *Rudolf Laban: An Extraordinary Life*, London: Dance Books.

Ratey, J. (2008) *SPARK: The revolutionary new science of exercise and the brain*, New York: Little, Brown & Co.

Sherborne, V. (2001) *Developmental Movement for Children* (2nd Edition), London: Worth Publishing Ltd.

Smith, A. (2004) 'The inclusion of pupils with special educational needs in secondary physical education', *Physical Education and Sport Pedagogy*, 9(1), 37–54.

Talbot, M. (2005) 'The physical literacy debate', *British Journal of Teaching Physical Education*, Autumn, 8–12.

Weston, C. (2008) *Physical Education in the Early Years: From praxis to axiology*, unpublished PhD thesis, University of Paisley.

Whitehead, M. (2001a) 'The concept of physical literacy', *European Journal of Physical Education*, 32(1), 127–138.

Whitehead, M. (2001b) 'The concept of physical literacy', *British Journal of Teaching Physical Education*, Spring, 32(1), 6–8.

Whitehead, M. (2004) 'Physical literacy – a debate'. Paper delivered at pre-Olympic Congress, Thessaloniki, Greece.

Whitehead, M. (2006) 'Physical literacy and physical education: conceptual mapping', *Physical Education Matters*, 1(1), 6–9.

Woodhead, M. (1989) 'School starts at five . . . or four years old? The rationale for changing admission policies in England and Wales', *Journal of Education Policy*, 4(1), 1–21.

Yelland, N. and Kilderry, A. (2005) 'Against the tide: new ways in early childhood education', in Yelland, N. (ed.) *Critical Issues in Education*, Berkshire: Open University Press.

5

Implications of special needs and multiculturalism for the early years curriculum

Prithvi Perepa

Overview

Autism spectrum disorders (ASD) are a common disability which early years practitioners will encounter in their professional life. This chapter focuses on how culture can influence the way families perceive a disability such as autism. It also covers a range of topics related to cultural perceptions, such as identification of autism, potential reactions from parents and its impact on the selection of skills to be taught within an early years curriculum. The chapter highlights issues to be considered while working with children on the autism spectrum belonging to minority ethnic communities and their families. With multiculturalism becoming the norm in most of the western world as well as other countries across the globe, it is important to consider the role of culture and special educational needs in providing an inclusive curriculum. The chapter ends with some reflective questions that will help you, as a practitioner, to connect these discussions to your own practice.

▶

Key Themes

- Differing cultural perceptions about autism and social behaviours.
- Impact of these perceptions on the families and practitioners.
- Strategies for supporting children from multicultural groups.

Introduction

The Early Years Foundation Stage framework (2012) in England states that pro-viding an inclusive curriculum is one of the objectives in an early years setting. While there are many aspects of inclusion, this chapter will discuss some of the cultural perceptions in relation to disability and special educational needs (SEN). Using autism as an example, this chapter will highlight a few of the issues that practitioners would need to be conscious of while delivering early years curriculum to children with SEN from minority ethnic communities and work-ing with their families.

Before we proceed it is important to understand how the term 'culture' is defined within this chapter. Culture can be defined as the distinctive way of life of a group, based on similar values (including child rearing and social relation-ships), religion and language (O'Hagan, 2001) which are learned, shared and transmitted from one generation to another (Mink, 1997). Children learn about their culture from a variety of sources: through routine exchanges and relation-ships between family members and families, from literature and media, through contacts with peers, and often through the differentiation of 'insiders' from 'outsiders' (Ahmad *et al.*, 1998). This could mean that what is considered as appropriate in one cultural context may not be so in a different one. With the increasing number of countries across the world becoming multicultural, it is important that sufficient attention is given to this while providing services to children and their families.

ASD is a developmental disability that impacts people in three main areas: social interaction, social communication and flexibility of thinking. These dif-ficulties are often termed the triad of impairments (Wing and Gould, 1979). The way autism affects an individual is variable. It is therefore commonly described as a spectrum condition since there can be children with autism who are unable to speak and interact with other people and may have learning difficulties, and children with normal intelligence and ability to speak but still influenced by the triad of impairments. For the purpose of this chapter, I will be using the term 'autism' to refer to the whole spectrum of the condition. Autism is considered to be one of the most common disabilities in the UK (Medical Research Council, 2001) and it is very likely that most nurseries and early years settings will come into contact with a child on the autism spectrum at some point.

As part of the early years curriculum, areas such as social skills, play skills and self-help skills are taught along with encouraging academic development. Plimley and Bowen (2007) contend that social skills learned by children with ASD in one setting are not automatically transferred to another. The difficulty in this kind of generalisation is not just limited to social skills, but almost all things that a child with autism learns. Even if these can be generalised, an important stage before teaching a set of skills is to find out their appropriateness to the individual's situation as it is possible families might have different expectations from those held by the educational professionals. In a multicultural society like the UK, where different cultural groups can have different sets of norms, this becomes especially pertinent. This is important as autism is diagnosed on the basis of behaviour exhibited by the individual. Therefore, it is essential to understand the cultural relevance attached to a particular behaviour before identifying a child with autism or any other special educational needs or disability.

Researchers have highlighted behaviour and skills that have been identified as appropriate or not in various cultures. O'Hagan (2001) mentions that, among Navajo Indians, making direct eye contact is an uncommon practice. Similar views have been expressed by researchers about Korean, Chinese, Japanese and Asian American cultures (John Lian, 1996; Le Roux, 2002; Park, 1996). Some Nigerian families I worked with also mentioned that direct eye contact is considered rude in their culture. It is possible that children from these cultures are taught by their parents and other family members not to give eye contact. However, this is often expected in western culture and in fact lack of eye contact is considered as one of the symptoms of the disorder when found in individuals with ASD. Its development is also encouraged in children as part of good listening skills in the early years curriculum.

Kim et al. (1997) mention that it is common and accepted in the Korean community to use elaborate language and indirect expressions in communication. In communities where an indirect style of communication is expected, using a direct style would be considered rude or inappropriate. In some other African communities it is considered rude to state a belief in the first person, hence the third person is often used for commentaries (Jamin, 1994). Unless the practitioners are sensitive to this, it is likely that they would think the child is unable to meet the curriculum's communication targets of expressing themselves even when opportunities are provided. Interestingly, using indirect language or referring to themselves in the third person is also associated with communication patterns displayed by people with ASD and can contribute to further confusion.

In her study on the interpretation of autism symptoms by parents in India, Daley (2004) has noticed differences among the various parents. While a mother was not alarmed that her son did not speak until he reached four years of age as 'boys speak late', a father thought his non-verbal son was dull-headed but would get better. These different perceptions could have an impact on whether or not a family considers these behaviours as difficulties that need to be addressed, which services they access, and when they do so. There is a possibility that some of these families may not be alarmed at the late speaking or lack of eye contact and may not seek help or follow the advice and intervention provided as they do not see the relevance.

Expanding on the idea of a cultural basis for observed behaviour, Wilder *et al.* (2004) add that behaviours such as tantrums, aggression, lack of 'normal' attachment to family members, lack of eye contact, poor social interaction and communication skills, and lack of emotional expression all have their roots in cultural differences and expectations. They provide the example of Asian-American children who may avoid eye contact with adults, and respond to teachers' questions by being silent out of respect for the adults. According to the authors, these behaviours could be interpreted by the school or early years staff, who are unaware of their cultural relevance, as difficulties in the areas of social skills and communication, and hence treated as possible symptoms of ASD. Sufficient awareness about cultural interpretations is therefore necessary before focusing on developing specific areas in communication or personal, social and emotional development in children from different cultural backgrounds.

Our perception of disability is influenced by our historical, religious and cultural background, which in turn affects our acceptance and understanding of the condition. Autism is rarely diagnosed before the age of three; this partly contributes to the development of a variety of theories about its causation within the families of these children as well as among professionals. Considering that ASDs are prevalent in all countries, one would expect to see a vast amount of research about these differences in the attitudes among the various countries and communities, but in reality there has been limited research on the subject. However, there is some research about how disability is understood and viewed in other cultures. This section will use this wider knowledge along with autism-specific information to provide an overview of the issue.

Khatleti *et al.* (1995) report that, in Lesotho, beliefs about the cause of disability were varied; some believed that being in contact with disabled people when a woman is pregnant could lead to her having a disabled child. Other views that were held included seeing disability as a result of eating protein during pregnancy, evil spirits, lack of attention to ancestral spirits, unfaithfulness during pregnancy, and misbehaviour in a previous life. The authors found that beliefs and practices around disability were based on varied sources of information, such as people's practical experiences, the need for survival, and ideas about general health.

Glidden *et al.* (1999) found that many Latino mothers who had children with disabilities considered witchcraft, fright or indigestion during pregnancy as possible contributors to their child's disability. Connors and Donnellan (1998) report that similar views regarding witchcraft as the reason for autism are held by the Navajo Indians. Dobson and Upadhyaya (2002), researching the Asian communities in the UK, found that some people believed that ASD could be caught by touching and was the result of children being neglected by working mothers and single parents. The authors found that the different groups within the Asian community had varying levels of knowledge. Urdu and Bengali speakers had limited understanding of the condition and felt that socialisation and social contact (including marriage) would improve the condition. It is important to consider these cultural perceptions of a disability as this will influence how the parents and the family view the child and how they will interact with different professionals.

It can be said that when people are unable to find answers they are likely to look for other explanations. Religion is another means of finding these answers. Religion can help some parents to cope with their child's diagnosis in a better way by providing an explanation and reducing their stress (Bennett et al., 1995; Rogers-Dulan, 1998; Tarakeshwar and Paragament, 2001), but it can also hinder the process (Glidden et al., 1999; Miles, 2002), for example where disability is seen as a punishment for sins committed in the current or previous life (Gabel, 2004; Liu, 2005). Researchers in the subject feel strongly that the role of religion in interpreting a condition and coping with it needs to be acknowledged in order to provide support and interventions that are culturally sensitive and appropriate. Although there can be situations where parents may say they only trust God to support their child, I have used the same language on some occasions with the parents, such as 'God helps those who help themselves', to engage them with the curriculum and the suggested strategies.

Every family is part of a society. This means that some of the values and attitudes held by the society at large could impact on individual family values. Cheng and Tang (1995) highlighted the impact of the society's attitude towards disability on families affected by it. They compared three groups of Chinese parents having children between four and six years with Down syndrome, language delay, and who were typically developing. They found that parents of children with Down syndrome withdrew from support and avoided taking their children to public places to escape stares, rejection or excessive sympathy reactions from others. They also found that fathers dealt with it differently and used avoidance to cope with distress. Although these experiences are limited to parents of very young children and may change as the child grows, this research highlights the fact that the attitudes of the community have their impact on how the family perceives disability. It is important to consider such issues and their impact on the families when thinking of involving parents and families in the learning process of the child. It is likely that parents who are ashamed of their child's condition may not even come to meetings or parents' evenings for fear of being judged.

Focusing on the social nature of disability and the differences of opinion among stakeholders, Mink (1997) states that in cultures that are not highly technological and do not need highly skilled labour, a child who is 'a bit slow' is not considered to have learning disabilities. Mink (ibid) further argues that the word 'retarded' or 'disabled' enters into these families' lives only when their children fail in American schools. Language is an important aspect with which to study a culture's attitude towards disability. For example, the American Indian languages do not have a word for disability. The terms used can be roughly translated as 'not completed yet' (Mink, 1997) and 'he's in his own world' (Connors and Donnellan, 1998). The words give an insight into how disability is perceived in these communities. Through my work with different communities I have also realised that most African and Asian languages do not have a word for ASD. The majority of people tend to favour the word that is used for learning disabilities or mental illness when referring to people with ASD. In fact, translated material about ASD provided by many organisations in the UK also used to use these words, which could further affect the attitudes that the family or the community holds towards the condition (Perepa, 2002).

However, it should not be considered that all minority ethnic groups have only negative or inappropriate attitudes towards people with disabilities and special educational needs. In fact, Kisanji (1995) criticises most of the research conducted into the attitudes of non-westerners regarding disabilities. He argues that western researchers have often written for a western audience, which can have its impact in understanding and presenting the research. He states that attitudes are best understood when different sources are used, such as proverbs, folk songs, folk tales and riddles. In his own research, where he used proverbs to understand attitudes, he found that these proverbs presented different attitudes that Tanzanians hold towards disabilities; for example, disability was represented as a source of inspiration for honesty, and it was believed that parents should take full responsibility for the care and upbringing of their child. Again this will influence the level of independence the family wants to develop in the child and when they think the child is mature enough to take responsibility for their actions, which can impact their perceptions of the importance teaching and learning of self-help skills in early years setting should have.

Acculturation of a family within the broader society can also influence a family's attitudes towards disability. By acculturation it is understood that a person will accept the means, tools and technology of the majority culture while retaining their own values (Joe, 1994). The views of members of a group can differ on the basis of the time and manner in which it has incorporated itself into a particular society (Greenfield, 1994). Harry (1992) says the process of acculturation may also differ on the basis of education and social class, with higher social class members and educated people finding it easier to do so. If this view is accepted then it has important implications when working with immigrant families from poorer socio-economic backgrounds.

Warner (1999) found in her study that opinions about what is the best option can differ among people from the same community. In her study of the Bangladeshi community living in the UK, she found that parents of children with severe learning disabilities differed in their views about how much the school should relate to their culture and speak to their children in Sylheti or Bangla. Similarly, some studies of parental views about the cause of autism have found that parents from various cultures may still hold similar perceptions about the cause of autism, such as immunisations, difficulties at birth or during pregnancy, and hereditary issues (Herbert and Koulouglioti, 2010; Perepa, 2008). Therefore, practitioners should not assume that all families from a particular culture have a specific opinion about the different curriculum areas. It is important to know how each family relates to their own cultural values and what the impact is in terms of their priorities for their child when it comes to early years curriculum areas.

For example, during a research study of Mexican families in the United States, Delgado-Gaitan (1994) found that there was a change in the way the parents interacted with their children. While they were involved in educational activities the children were encouraged to interact, as this was considered a necessary skill for academic progress in the US, but in daily family activities children were still expected to respect adults and asking questions was considered rebellious. Further, Delgado-Gaitan (1994) mentions that immigrant Mexican families mainly encouraged interdependence, whereas the first-generation Mexican families encouraged independence as well as interdependence. They made compromises so that their children learned both sets of values, to fit the family and the wider society. The children in this study do not have autism. It might be difficult for children with ASD to adapt according to the situation because of the difficulties they have with generalisation of skills. This makes it even more important to involve the parents in selecting the targets that are considered appropriate for the child in both settings.

There is a significant group of researchers in the field of disabilities who argue that the concept of disabilities is a social construct (Dudley-Marling, 2004; Wolkind and Rutter, 1985). Because of this there could be variance in the way any disability is understood in different cultures. There is also an increasing agreement in the field of disabilities that constructs such as 'adaptive behaviour' or 'challenging behaviour' are the result of an interaction between the person and their environment (Hatton, 2002). In fact, this is the case for any social behaviour. Any behaviour is considered socially appropriate or not on the basis of what is expected in that environment. Culture inevitably forms a major part of the environment. This same argument of social construct can also be used in relation to the early years curriculum as there is no universal agreement about what is considered to be the norm or important for children to learn across the world, as the other chapters in this book illustrate. Areas chosen within the curriculum are often influenced by the assumed norms of specific people within the given society.

Harry and Kalyanpur (1994) state that families from minority ethnic communities may embrace a wider definition of 'normalcy' than that accepted by educational professionals in school settings. Yamamoto et al. (1997) argue that there is potential for misunderstanding culturally appropriate behaviours and diagnosing them as psychological disorders. Therefore, it becomes important that culture is considered when providing services. This ensures that what is measured or taught is socially relevant and avoids misdiagnosis due to cultural reasons. It has also been suggested that students from different cultural backgrounds experience more difficulties with behaviour customs and school expectations (Dyches et al., 2004). This again could be because of the different accepted norms in the two settings.

Influence of culture on practitioners and curriculum priorities

Culture not only influences a family's perception but can also influence what professionals consider as appropriate in a given context. A study conducted by Mandell et al. (2009) in the US found disparities in the kind of diagnosis that children from different ethnic backgrounds were being given and that it was less likely for Black and Hispanic children to receive a diagnosis of ASD compared with White boys. In an earlier survey conducted by Cucasso et al. (1996) on the attitudes of professionals (speech and language therapists, school psychologists and physicians in child psychiatry) towards ASD and how these can be formed on the basis of ethnic and social background, the results showed that although ethnicity did not play a role in influencing the perceptions of the professionals, the socio-economic status (SES) of the family did influence their perception. For example, given the same vignette, those from a low SES family were often diagnosed with cultural deprivation, whereas those from a high SES family were diagnosed with autism. Even though the research found no differences with regards to ethnicity, this highlights how professionals' decisions can be influenced by their previous knowledge and attitudes. This may not be limited to diagnosing ASD but could extend to how interventions are designed and which areas are prioritised. It is important that you, as an early years practitioner, are aware of your own cultural beliefs and values and how they may impact your perception of the behaviours of others.

Teaching social communication skills is an important part of the curriculum for children on the autism spectrum. Many early years settings spend time teaching these children to understand facial expressions and emotions. Woodhead et al. (1995) mention that there are cultural differences in attitudes towards various emotional expressions and their acceptability. From my own experience I am aware that in some traditional Indian families it is not considered appropriate for females in the house to laugh in front of older male members of the family. In such situations, not smiling or laughing does not mean the person is not happy, but the expression is restricted due to its acceptability in the society. Similarly, in the Chinese community a smile does not always indicate happiness but could mean embarrassment or feeling shy (Liu, 2005). This kind of knowledge is vital when teaching topics such as emotions to children with autism from minority ethnic communities. Culture and language abilities can also impact on alternative communication systems used by the children. For example, if a child is using a voice output system which can give information in English only and some of the family members do not have sufficient English comprehension to understand these requests, it can actually lead to frustration on both sides (Tincani et al., 2009) and perhaps even to exhibition of challenging behaviours by the child.

There is also a dearth of research about parental expectations and priorities with regards to the curriculum for children with ASD from different cultural groups. In a study conducted by Lim et al. (2000), the researchers interviewed 77 parents in Singapore about the areas they prioritise for teaching their disabled children. They found that these caregivers valued teaching self-help skills more than other functional, social or academic skills. They also found that parents who had children with mild or moderate disabilities rated social relationships skills higher than did parents of children with moderate and severe disabilities. Although there are some limitations with this study, what is worth noting is that if there are differences in priorities between the parents and professionals, it would be unlikely that the parents would follow the professionals' suggestions at home. This, in effect, can send confused messages to a child with autism and make learning and consolidation of skills difficult for them.

Commenting on the importance of being aware of the cultural differences, Miles (2002) argues that suitable services and resources cannot be developed unless a good understanding of people's cultures and their concepts of disability has been developed by the professionals. Dyches et al. (2007) express similar views and highlight the importance of having social interaction goals that are appropriate to the child and its culture. This makes it necessary to involve the family when deciding which symbols need to be used for children with autism in alternative means of communication such as the Picture Exchange System or other visual-based systems. The interaction of the parents with their child, how they perceive their role as a parent and that of a professional are also based on cultural expectations (Fung and Roseberry-McKibbin, 1999; Hwa-Froelich and Vigil, 2004; Rodriguez and Olswang, 2003; Vigil and Hwa-Froelich, 2004; Wilder et al., 2004). For example, some parents may expect professionals to provide more directed interventions and may not appreciate the role of problem solving or learning through discovery. Where professionals are encouraging their children to participate in such activities, they may consider that valuable time is being wasted. Hence, it is important to understand the family attitudes towards autism and what they consider as important skills for their children, and how they perceive their own role and that of the professionals to be able to develop interventions that are culturally sensitive and appropriate. It has been found that lack of culturally appropriate services can lead families to disengage from the available services (Perepa, 2007).

It is also important that this knowledge is then not generalised to all the families from that cultural group. As Hatton (2002) suggests, ethnicity should not be considered as a monolithic construct; rather, it is necessary to identify which aspects of ethnicity are considered to be important by different members of the community. He also says that there are many other sources of cultural variation across individuals other than ethnicity, such as social class, language and nationality. Rogers-Dulan and Blacher (1995) suggested a conceptual framework that can help in understanding how a family adjusts to a disability. The factors that they have identified as important to consider are culture, ethnicity, religious affiliation, family structure and functions. They suggest all these factors impact on how a family interprets their role, finds coping strategies and adjusts to a disability. They also point out that each family may differ in the amount that these factors can influence them. Glidden et al. (1999) extend this model to include neighbourhood, school system, friends, economic system and macro-cultural values.

It is important that early years professionals consider all these factors as far as possible when delivering curriculum to children with special educational needs.

Reflective Questions

1. What will you do if a family you are working with has different ideas about the age for reaching developmental milestones compared with your own views about the expected age?

2. Are you aware of your own bias about different cultural or religious groups and its implications to your work with children and their families?

3. What is your understanding of how the families you work with view their role and your own in supporting the child?

4. Which skills do they feel are important for their child to acquire?

5. How do families you work with view their child's disability or special educational needs? How could you use this knowledge in engaging the families with your setting?

References

Ahmad, W., Darr, A., Jones, L. and Nisar, G. (1998) *Deafness and Ethnicity*, Bristol: The Policy Press.

Bennett, T., Deluca, D. A. and Allen, R. W. (1995) 'Religion and children with disabilities', *Journal of Religion and Health*, 34(4), 301–312.

Cheng, P. and Tang, C. S. (1995) 'Coping and psychological distress of Chinese parents with Down syndrome', *Mental Retardation*, 33(1), 10–20.

Connors, J. L. and Donnellan, A. M. (1998) 'Walk in beauty: Western perspectives on disability and Navajo family/cultural resilience', in McCubbin, H. I., Thompson, E. A., Thompson, I. A. and Fromer, J. E. (eds.) *Resiliency in Native American Immigrant Families*, Thousand Oaks, CA: Sage Publications.

Cucasso, M. L., Wright, H. H., Rownd, C. V., Abramson, R. K., Waller, J. and Fender, D. (1996) 'Brief report: professional perceptions of children with developmental difficulties: The influence of race and socioeconomic status', *Journal of Autism and Developmental Disorders*, 26(4), 461–469.

Daley, T. C. (2004) 'From symptom recognition to diagnosis: children with autism in urban India', *Social Science and Medicine*, 58(7), 1323–1335.

Delgado-Gaitan, C. (1994) 'Socializing young children in Mexican-American families: an intergenerational perspective', in Greenfield, P. M. and Cocking, R. R. (eds.) *Cross-cultural Roots of Minority Child Development*, Hillsdale, NJ: Lawrence Erlbaum Associates.

Department for Education (2012) *Statutory Framework for Early Years Foundation Stage*, Cheshire: Department for Education.

Dobson, S. and Upadhyaya, S. (2002) 'Concepts of autism in Asian communities in Bradford, UK', *Good Autism Practice*, 3(2), 43–51.

Dudley-Marling, C. (2004) 'The social construction of learning disabilities', *Journal of Learning Disabilities*, 37(6), 482–489.

Dyches, T. T., Wilder, L. K., Algozzine, B. and Obiakor, F. E. (2007) 'Working with multicultural learners with autism', in Obiakor, F. E. (ed.) *Multicultural special Education: Culturally responsive teaching*, Upper Saddle River, NJ: Pearson.

Dyches, T. T., Wilder, L. K., Sudweeks, R. R., Obiakor, F. E. and Algozzine, B. (2004) 'Multicultural issues in autism', *Journal of Autism and Developmental Disorders*, 34(2), 211–222.

Fung, F. and Roseberry-McKibbin, C. (1999) 'Service delivery in working with clients from Cantonese-speaking backgrounds', *American Journal of Speech-Language Pathology*, 8(4), 309–318.

Gabel, S. (2004) 'South Asian Indian cultural orientation towards mental retardation', *Mental Retardation*, 42(1), 12–25.

Glidden, L. M., Rogers-Dulan, J. and Hill, A. E. (1999) ' "The child that was meant?" or "punishment for sin?"; Religion, ethnicity, and families with children with disabilities', *International Review of Research in Mental Retardation*, 22, 267–288.

Greenfield, P. M. (1994) 'Independence and interdependence as developmental scripts: implications for theory, research, and practice', in Greenfield, P. M. and Cocking, R. R. (eds.) *Cross-cultural Roots of Minority Child Development*, Hillsdale, NJ: Lawrence Erlbaum Associates.

Harry, B. (1992) *Cultural Diversity, Families and Special Education System*, New York: Teachers College Press.

Harry, B. and Kalyanpur, M. (1994) 'Cultural underpinnings of special education: implications for professional interactions with culturally diverse families', *Disability and Society*, 9(2), 145–165.

Hatton, C. (2002) 'People with intellectual disabilities from ethnic minority communities in the United States and the United Kingdom', *International Review of Research in Mental Retardation*, 25, pp. 209–239.

Herbert, E. and Koulouglioti, C. (2010) 'Parental beliefs about cause and course of their child's autism and outcomes of their beliefs: a review of the literature', *Issues in Comprehensive Paediatric Nursing*, 33(3), 149–163.

Hwa-Froelich, D. A. and Vigil, D. C. (2004) 'Three aspects of cultural influence on communication', *Communication Disorders Quarterly*, 25(3), 107–118.

Jamin, J. R. (1994) 'Language and socialization of the child in African families living in France', in Greenfield, P. M. and Cocking, R. R. (eds.) *Cross-cultural Roots of Minority Child Development*, Hillsdale, NJ: Lawrence Erlbaum Associates.

Joe, J. R. (1994) 'Revaluing Native American concepts of development and education', in Greenfield, P. M. and Cocking, R. R. (eds.) *Cross-cultural Roots of Minority Child Development*, Hillsdale, NJ: Lawrence Erlbaum Associates.

John Lian, M. (1996) 'Teaching Asian American children', in Duran, E. (ed.) *Teaching Students with Moderate/Severe Disabilities, Including Autism* (2nd Edition), Springfield, IL: Charles Thomas.

Khatleti, P., Mariga, L., Phachaka, L. and Stubbs, S. (1995) 'Schools for all: national planning in Lesotho', in O'Toole, B. and McConkey, R. (eds.) *Innovations in Developing Countries for People with Disabilities*, Lancashire: Lisieux Hall.

Kim, W. J., Kim, L. I. and Rue, D. S. (1997) 'Korean American children', in Johnson-Powell, G. and Yamamoto, J. (eds.) *Transcultural Child Development – Psychological Assessment and Treatment*, New York: John Wiley & Sons.

Kisanji, J. (1995) 'Attitudes and beliefs about disability in Tanzania', in O'Toole, B. and McConkey, R. (eds.) *Innovations in Developing Countries for People with Disabilities*, Lancashire: Lisieux Hall.

Le Roux, J. (2002) 'Effective educators are culturally competent communicators', *Intercultural Education*, 13(1), 37–48.

Lim, L., Girl, T. A. and Quah, M. M. (2000) 'Singaporean parents' curriculum priorities for their children with disabilities', *International Journal of Disability, Development and Education*, 47(1), 77–87.

Liu, G. Z. (2005). 'Developing cross-cultural competence from a Chinese perspective', in Stone, J. H. (ed.) *Culture and Disability: Providing culturally competent services*, pp. 65–85, Thousand Oaks, CA: Sage Publications.

Mandell, D., Wiggins, L., Carpenter, L., Daniels, J., DiGuiseppi, C., Durkin, M., Giarelli, E., Morrier, M., Nicholas, J., Pinto-Martin, J., Shattuck, P., Thomas, K., Yeargin-Allsopp, M. and Kirty, R. (2009) 'Racial/Ethnic disparities in the identification of children with autism spectrum disorders', *American Journal of Public Health*, 99(3), 493–498.

Medical Research Council (2001) *MRC Review of Autism Research: Epidemiology and causes*, London: Medical Research Council.

Miles, M. (2002) 'Some influences of religions on attitudes towards disabilities and people with disabilities', *Journal of Religion, Disability and Health*, 6(2–3), 117–129.

Mink, T. (1997) 'Studying culturally diverse families of children with mental retardation-IRIS', *International Review of Research in Mental Retardation*, 20, 75–98.

O'Hagan, K. (2001) *Cultural Competence in the Caring Professions*, London: Jessica Kingsley.

Park, H. (1996) 'Korean-American families of children with disabilities; perspectives and implications for practitioners', in Duran, E. (ed.) *Teaching Students with Moderate/Severe Disabilities, Including Autism* (2nd Edition), Springfield, IL: Charles Thomas.

Perepa, P. (2002) 'Issues in accessing support for families with a child with an ASD from the Indian Sub-Continent living in the United Kingdom', *Good Autism Practice*, 3(2), 52–71.

Perepa, P. (2007) 'Are ASD services accessible for minority ethnic communities?', *Good Autism Practice*, 8(2), 3–8.

Perepa, P. (2008) 'Cultural perceptions about autism spectrum disorders and social behaviour: a qualitative study', unpublished PhD thesis, University of Birmingham.

Plimley, L. and Bowen, M. (2007) *Social Skills and Autistic Spectrum Disorders*, London: Sage Publications.

Rodriguez, B. L. and Olswang, L. B. (2003) 'Mexican-American and Anglo-American mothers' beliefs and values about child rearing, education, and language impairment', *American Journal of Speech-Language Pathology*, 12, 452–462.

Rogers-Dulan, J. (1998) 'Religious connectedness among urban African-American families who have a child with disabilities', *Mental Retardation*, 36(2), 91–103.

Rogers-Dulan, J. and Blacher, J. (1995) 'African American families, religion, and disability: A conceptual framework', *Mental Retardation*, 33(4), 226–238.

Tarakeshwar, N. and Paragament, K. I. (2001) 'Religious coping in families of children with autism', *Focus on Autism and other Developmental Disabilities*, 16(4), 247–260.

Tincani, M., Travers, J. and Boutot, A. (2009) 'Race, culture and autism spectrum disorder: Understanding the role of diversity in successful educational interventions', *Research & Practice for Persons with Severe Disabilities*, 34(3–4), 81–90.

Vigil, D. C. and Hwa-Froelich, D. A. (2004) 'Interaction styles in minority caregivers: Implications for intervention', *Communication Disorders Quarterly*, 25(3), 119–126.

Warner, R. (1999) 'The views of Bangladeshi parents on the special school attended by their young children with severe learning difficulties', *British Journal of Special Education*, 26(4), 218–223.

Wilder, L. K., Dyches, T. T., Obiakor, F. E. and Algozzine, B. (2004) 'Multicultural perspectives on teaching students with autism', *Focus on Autism and Other Developmental Disabilities*, 19(2), 105–113.

Wing, L. and Gould, J. (1979) 'Severe impairments of social interaction and associated abnormalities in children: epidemiology and classification', *Journal of Autism and Developmental Disabilities*, 9(1), 11–29.

Wolkind, S. and Rutter, M. (1985) 'Social-cultural factors', in Rutter, M. and Hersov, L. (eds.) *Child and Adolescent Psychiatry – Modern Approaches*, Oxford: Blackwell.

Woodhead, M., Barnes, P., Miell, D. and Oates, J. (1995) 'Developmental perspectives on emotion', in Barnes, P. (ed.) *Personal, Social and Emotional Development of Children*, Milton Keynes: Open University.

Yamamoto, J., Silva, J. A., Ferrari, M. and Nukariya, K. (1997) 'Culture and psychopathology', in Jonson-Powell, G. and Yamamoto, J. (eds.) *Transcultural Child Development – Psychological Assessment and Treatment*, New York: John Wiley and Sons.

6

A book is a machine: electronic storybooks in the early years curriculum

John Trushell

Overview

The early years curriculum has been criticised as lacking a clear strategy concerning information and communication technology (ICT) in general and children's emergent digital literacy practices in particular (Marsh, 2007a). The most recent framework for the Early Years Foundation Stage (DfE, 2012), for instance, addresses ICT as an aspect in the specific area 'Understanding the World' and expresses the broad expectation that children will 'recognise that a range of technology is used in places such as homes and schools' and be able to 'select and use technology for particular purposes' (ibid, p. 9). However, the statutory framework does not explicitly address – either in the prime area of Communication and Language or in the specific area of Literacy – the issue of ICT in communication, language or literacy.

Moreover, the early years framework places emphasis on reading which privileges the use of phonic knowledge (ibid, p. 8), an emphasis heightened by the announcement of a Year 1 phonics screening check 'to confirm whether individual children have learnt phonic decoding to an appropriate standard' (STA, 2012, p. 2). The conventional approach to phonics, and to synthetic phonics in particular, can be restrictive and prescriptive insofar as these prioritise, first and foremost, an appropriate command of phonics before tackling an actual book. However, the framework does stipulate that 'children must be given access to a wide range of reading materials . . . to ignite their interest' (DfE, 2012, p. 5) and this chapter contends that the range of reading materials should include electronic illustrated storybooks, a term denoting those reading programmes available for a range of platforms, from learning-aid consoles to personal computers. These electronic storybooks can be reconciled with the early years curriculum.

Key Themes

- Effects of environmental print awareness and adult–child storybook reading.
- Effects of informal and formal adult–child storybook reading.
- Potential of adult–child media engagement with electronic storybooks.

Sharing storybooks

When the eminent 20th-century literary critic I. A. Richards observed, in the preface of *Principles of Literary Criticism* (1924, p. 1), that 'a book is a machine to think with', his remark was made in the context of literature – the implication being that 'literature itself is a technology, a way of accomplishing something for writers and readers' (Goodwyn, 2000, p. 2) – rather than in the context of literacy. Nevertheless, the metaphor of a book as a machine has implications for the acquisition of literacy.

A book is a machine insofar as print technologises the spoken word (Ong, 1982, p. 80). The spoken word draws on a set of biological endowments (Everett, 2012, p. 89), including tongue, teeth, throat and lungs, while the written word requires implements, such as a stylus, a quill or a pen, and materials such as clay, papyrus and paper. Thus, literacy is technological and not naturally acquired by children but must be culturally transmitted (Grabe and Kaplan, 1996, p. 6). Literacy in literate societies is transmitted to children by observation of or by participation in literacy activities (Justice and Kaderavek, 2002, p. 8).

Opportunities to observe and participate in literacy activities are provided by shared storybook reading: a child and a trusted adult sharing a storybook in the idealised and iconic bedtime story routine (Anderson *et al.*, 2010, p. 39) or an adult, such as a teacher or a librarian, acting as a storyteller, presenting a storybook to children. Storybook reading is a reassuringly predictable social process, providing an ideal context in which to develop children's awareness of print, breadth of vocabulary and command of story grammar (McLachlan, 2007, p. 21).

Other than storybook reading, commonplace childhood literacy events demonstrate children's awareness of print, including:

- selecting a cold bathroom tap by a logographic 'C' and selecting toothpaste, e.g. Colgate, by label (Hallet, 1999, p. 55);
- scanning a cereal packet at the breakfast table, consolidating the logographic 'K' of Kellogg's, or spotting in the street the golden arches logographic 'M' on the storefront of McDonald's (see Cronin *et al.*, 1999);
- recognising name tags at nursery, playgroup or preschool by applying logographic knowledge to companions' names, e.g. discerning 'K' and 'M' in 'KIM' or 'M', 'C' and 'K' in 'MICK' (Riley, 1998, p. 56);
- applying logographic knowledge when labelling or signing artwork (Trushell, 1998a);
- following signs encountered in the street – 'STOP' and 'WALK' – or instructions on home appliances, e.g. 'ON'/'OFF' (see Orellana and Hernández, 1999);
- applying logographic knowledge when composing stage properties for play, e.g. a song sheet or a wall chart (Trushell, 1998b).

Although these commonplace activities may indicate print awareness, research has indicated that environmental print awareness and 'pretend writing' should not be considered as precursors of reading (Justice, 2006, p. 290): environmental print awareness is a limited predictor of 'later reading skills or other later emergent literacy skills' such as 'letter knowledge and phonological sensitivity' (Lonigan *et al.*, 2000, p. 610). However, frequency of adult–child storybook reading predicts between 15 per cent and 24 per cent of the variance of young children's print awareness, considered a prerequisite for word reading (Justice *et al.*, 2005, p. 231), and directly predicts nursery vocabulary and the frequency with which children report reading for pleasure in primary later years (Sénéchal, 2006, p. 83).

Adult–child storybook reading is conventionally considered as being 'entrenched within the sociocultural lives of middle-class groups' (Marsh, 2003, p. 370) and the Alliance for Childhood, based in the United States, has advocated 'a solid introduction to books, which most middle-class children have from infancy onwards' (Miller and Almon, 2006, p. 8), 'via good books read aloud' (ibid, p. 58), consistent with a belief that 'reading books aloud with favourite adults is especially crucial for young children' (Cordes and Miller, 2004, p. 74).

The emphasis on dialogic reading – books read aloud by trusted adults and children – is intended to improve 'the oral language and listening comprehension abilities of young children' (Chambers *et al.*, 2010, p. 36). Research has confirmed that:

> children's literacy skills are enhanced when parents engage them in direct literacy and language enriching activities like joint book reading, playing rhyming games, singing songs, and drawing.
>
> (Weigel et al., 2010, p. 6)

There is a strong correlation between parents' active and direct engagement with their child in activities designed to foster literacy or language development, e.g. rhyming games and shared reading, and the child's oral language, phonological sensitivity, letter-sound knowledge and word decoding (Burgess *et al.*, 2002, p. 421). However, shared reading may be categorised as formal and informal:

- Adult–child storybook reading, focusing on the text and pictures in the book, during which the adult poses questions, expands on the meaning of words, provides definitions, responds to the child's questions and repeats exposure to specific books is categorised as informal interaction.
- Adult–child storybook reading, focusing directly on the written language in the book, during which the adult teaches the child about letters by providing the name of the letter and the sound of specific letters, is categorised as formal interaction (Sénéchal, 2006, p. 60; Sénéchal and LeFevre, 2002, p. 446).

Research has indicated that 'informal interactions with print . . . were related to the development of receptive language' while 'more formal interactions with print . . . were related to the development of emergent literacy' (Sénéchal and LeFevre, 2002, p. 447). While engagement in informal storybook reading predicts nursery vocabulary and reading for pleasure in primary later years, engagement in formal storybook reading directly predicts nursery alphabet knowledge, first-year primary reading and reading fluency in primary later years (Sénéchal, 2006, p. 83). Informal interactions should precede formal interactions, but both are necessary if children are to become articulate and to acquire literacy (see Figure 6.1). Reviewing research on shared storybook reading, Phillips *et al.* (2008, p. 87) concluded:

> The chief possibility of shared-book reading is that, supplemented with explicitly teaching children about print, it has proven benefits for future reading ability.

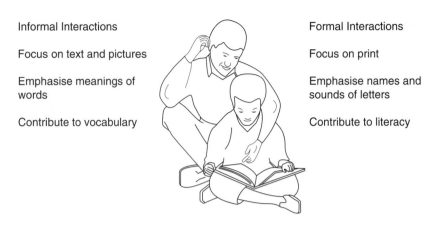

Informal Interactions	Formal Interactions
Focus on text and pictures	Focus on print
Emphasise meanings of words	Emphasise names and sounds of letters
Contribute to vocabulary	Contribute to literacy

Figure 6.1 Informal and formal shared storybook reading

Effectively, research has shown that a child's language and literacy experiences before their second birthday strongly influence their performance at school entry (Roulstone *et al.*, 2011, p. 1).

Sharing electronic storybooks

Those adults who engage in adult–child storybook reading, perhaps mindful of their responsibility as 'gatekeepers' – 'safeguarding children from media's potentially harmful effects' (Wartella and Jennings, 2000, p. 34) – have tended to mistrust those literacy practices that children experience beyond this context (Marsh, 2006, p. 35; Marsh, 2007b, p. 267) and have tended to be cautious of each new medium – cinema, radio, television, ICT – that might challenge the primacy of print. Such mistrust may be attributed in part to authoritative publications that have decried these media. The educational psychologist Jane Healy, for instance, published *Endangered Minds: Why children don't think and what we can do about it* (1990), an indictment of television and video games for adversely affecting children's cognitive and linguistic development, and *Failure to Connect: How computers affect our children's minds and what we can do about it* (1998), an indictment of ICT for adversely affecting children's cognitive, emotional and linguistic development. However, with reference to Healy, Cuban (2001, p. 62) remarked that many authorities:

> believe in early childhood as a critical period for becoming literate, and they have few doubts about either the appropriateness or effectiveness of young children in preschools or kindergartens working on computers with software matched to their age.

However, the appropriateness of ICT in early childhood has continued to be challenged by those who contend that such technologies are not conducive to children's development socially, physically, intellectually, linguistically and emotionally. The Alliance for Childhood published *Fool's Gold* (Cordes and Miller, 2000), an indictment of new technologies as engaging children in sedentary and solitary activities detrimental to health and learning (Plowman and Stephen, 2003, p. 151; Reynolds *et al.*, 2003, p. 153). While the Alliance for Childhood has contended that any technology should be simple and should not intrude between the child and the activities of reading and writing (Cordes and Miller, 2004, p. 78), this contention could be considered not only as technophobic but also as privileging those middle-class literacy practices inherent in a solid introduction to good books.

Despite the misgivings of authorities such as Healy and pressure groups such as the Alliance for Childhood, reading electronic illustrated storybooks has become an increasingly common early literacy event in the home lives of many children. These storybooks have been marketed as electronic learning aids (ELA) by manufacturers who claim that their products are 'superior platforms for children's learning compared to television, especially because of their interactive nature' (Wartella *et al.*, 2004, p. 5).

An independent appraisal of the potential of electronic storybooks to support the development of children's literacy concluded that the best of these storybooks combined multimedia and interactive additions, including highlighting of text while the text is narrated, animation of illustrations and cued animation and sound effects, in such a way that the additions each support aspects of literacy whether at home or in kindergarten (de Jong and Bus, 2003, p. 161).

Research in the US has shown that three out of four parents (76 per cent) reported that their children had such storybooks (Rideout *et al.*, 2003, p. 9). Research commissioned by the Kaiser Family Foundation (KFF) reported that parents were convinced that such toys had benefits:

> Nearly two-thirds (62%) of parents say educational toys like talking books are "very important'" to children's intellectual development.
>
> (Garrison and Christakis, 2005, p. 23)

Research in Scotland similarly reported that children were 'enthusiastic users' of electronic illustrated storybooks and that 'parents were convinced of their educational value' (McPake *et al.*, 2005, 18).

Electronic illustrated storybooks can be accommodated within the conventional model of adult–child shared reading – joint media engagement (JME), a term coined by the Media and Learning Group at Stanford Research Institute, includes shared reading with either digital or traditional media. A small-scale study of a mother engaging in shared reading of conventional and electronic storybooks with her sons indicated that storybook format influenced parent–child interactions (Kim and Anderson, 2008, p. 237). The study observed that the children reading an electronic book engaged in greater non-immediate talk, i.e. making comments, posing questions about general knowledge and drawing inferences and predicting, than immediate talk, posing questions about the text and illustrations, compared with the conventional book. Further research comparing adult–child shared reading of conventional and electronic storybooks has indicated that the medium can affect interaction with the text. A study of 25 preschool children reading conventional and electronic storybooks with research assistants indicated that the preschool children ask twice as many labelling questions (e.g. 'What is that?') when reading conventional storybooks, and that these children demonstrated significantly higher levels of persistence with the task of reading when reading the electronic storybook (Moody *et al.*, 2010, p. 306). A further study of 128 kindergarten children indicated that children who had participated in shared electronic storybook reading with an adult demonstrated greater progress in developing concepts about print (CAP), word reading and phonological awareness than those children who had shared a conventional storybook with an adult (Segal-Drori *et al.*, 2010, p. 924).

A further perceived advantage of these storybooks is that such ELAs may also offer opportunities for children to read independently, providing respite from childcare for parents to engage in 'domestic tasks or leisure activities' (Plowman *et al.*, 2008, p. 310). However, researchers have cautioned that the provision of an electronic book for children to read with minimal intervention by adults may merely provide entertainment: the electronic book will not function as a surrogate adult (Trushell *et al.*, 2001, p. 400). The comparative study that featured 128 kindergarten children also examined children who had shared an electronic storybook with an adult and children who read an electronic storybook alone. Those children who had read with an adult demonstrated greater progress in developing CAP, word reading and phonological awareness (Segal-Drori *et al.*, 2010).

Adult mediation of storybooks for young children is essential to children's language and literacy development. Such mediation assists a child to read beyond their independent capability: the adult mediation is fostering not only fundamental language skills – print awareness, word reading and phonological awareness – but also knowledge of discourse conventions, appreciation of the purpose and goals of reading, and acquisition of general knowledge (see Figure 6.2).

The intention of adult mediation is that the child will develop the multiplicity of skills and the variety of knowledge required to handle print technology.

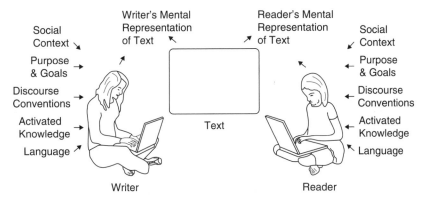

Figure 6.2 A model of discourse construction (adapted from Flower, 1994, p. 53)

Interactive books in early years curriculum

Jackie Marsh, in the article 'New literacies and old pedagogies' (2007b), remarked a disconcerting divergence between those new literacy practices in which children engage outside of schools and the literacy curricula and pedagogy legislated for children by policy makers. A recent review of technology and literacy in early childhood educational settings contends that national policies concerning early literacy have 'implied conflicting messages about the relationship between technology and literacy' (Burnett, 2010, p. 248) and stresses the urgent need for those responsible for curricula and pedagogy:

> to understand better the possibilities for integrating new technologies within early literacy provision, and gain informed insights about children's experience and response to such opportunities.

An early appraisal of the potential of electronic storybooks for use with beginning readers concluded that 'prudent use clearly holds great potential for supplementing what teachers do to foster literacy growth' (McKenna *et al.*, 1996, p. 6), and recent research has confirmed that electronic story books can supplement conventional literacy interactions (Sénéchal, 2006; Sénéchal and LeFevre, 2002):

- informal activities, focusing on the text and pictures in the book, during which the child poses questions, infers, comments and predicts (Kim and Anderson, 2008);
- formal activities, focusing directly on the written language in the book, during which the child consolidates or develops concepts about print, word reading and phonological awareness (Segal-Drori *et al.*, 2010).

Paradoxically, this new technology is supplementary and does not radically challenge old pedagogy: commentators – and critics – have remarked that electronic books 'are the most obvious connection to a traditional literacy model using conventions associated with reading books' (Gamble, 2000, p. 4), although this retention of a conventional storybook format and potential assimilation into existing pedagogical practices could be advantageous (Trushell and Maitland, 2005, p. 65).

Early years practitioners could use JME with individual readers and, via a monitor or an interactive whiteboard, with groups of readers consistent with the conventional practice of shared reading conventional storybooks with individuals and big books with groups. The reported contention that electronic books 'could provide an effective substitute for adults when none was available' (Lankshear and Knobel, 2003, p. 70) would not realise the potential of JME and shared reading for supporting beginning readers, but Cuban (2001, p. 63) has reported, in a US context:

> Popular stories that in a pre-computer age early childhood teachers would read to their children during circle-time, for example, have been made into [electronic storybooks] that are bought by districts and sent to classrooms.

Nevertheless, as noted in a report to the Department for Education and Skills, electronic books have not 'become quite the force that was expected' (Cox *et al.*, 2003, p. 23). Although the potential of electronic books was reaffirmed in *Informing Practice in English* (Myhill and Fisher, 2005, p. 11), a report commissioned by the Office for Standards in Education (Ofsted), recent interviews with 51 Early Years Foundation Stage practitioners working across a range of local authorities in England and Wales reported that only one practitioner mentioned the use of electronic storybooks (Aubrey and Dahl, 2008, p. 75).

The reported reluctance of early years practitioners to use electronic storybooks with beginning readers may be attributable to the prioritisation of learning reading by conventional approaches, such as synthetic phonics, and a reliance upon traditional practices which privilege decoding of alphabetic print (Marsh, 2007a) – priorities and practices which predominate in current literacy policy directions (Lankshear and Knobel, 2003, p. 77) – but practitioners probably 'need to broaden their definition of "beginning reading" and all that that entails' (Turbill, 2001, p. 277). Such positions concerning electronic books and reading are becoming 'increasingly anachronistic' (Burnett, 2010, p. 265) and potential benefits for pupils are being limited by outmoded pedagogical beliefs (Webb and Cox, 2004, p. 252). Recent research has concluded that electronic books which incorporate multimedia and interactive features – highlighting of text

Reflective Questions

1. When anticipating engagement in shared reading with individual children and/or groups of children, how does one prepare (e.g. prompts and questions) to promote formal and informal interactions related to the text and pictures?

2. Having engaged in shared reading with individual children as part of the curriculum, how does one monitor (or record) these interactions (formal or informal)?

3. What criteria should be applied when considering electronic storybook features – e.g. text highlighting while the text is narrated, animation of illustrations, and cued animation and sound effects – which may support formal and informal interactions in the delivery of the curriculum?

4. When engaging in joint media engagement with individual children and/or groups of children, how does one promote formal and informal interactions related to all features of the text, e.g. text highlighting, text narration, animation and cued animation and sound effects?

while the text is narrated, animation of illustrations, and cued animation and sound effects – have the capacity to 'increase children's comprehension and enjoyment of storybooks' (Grimshaw *et al.*, 2007, p. 598). Moreover, research has indicated that electronic books have the potential to support the literacy development of pupils at risk: children with lower levels of language proficiency, such as pupils with English as an Additional Language, particularly benefited from reading electronic books (Verhallen *et al.*, 2006, p. 417–418) and the emergent literacy levels of pupils with lower socio-economic status showed relatively greater improvement rates than did the literacy levels of children with middle socio-economic status (Korat and Shamir, 2008).

Unless early years practitioners use electronic storybooks in classrooms, the probable beneficiaries of electronic storybooks will be those children who use these electronic learning aids at home and who are not children customarily at risk of reading failure. Thus, 'the gap between those who have daily use of books with technology in the home and those who do not' will widen (Kempster, 2000, p. 28). When a book is a machine literally, not merely metaphorically, beginning readers at risk of reading disadvantage are placed in double jeopardy.

References

Anderson, J., Anderson, A., Friedrich, N. and Kim, J. (2010) 'Taking stock of family literacy: some contemporary perspectives', *Journal of Early Childhood Literacy*, 10(1), 33–53.

Aubrey, C. and Dahl, S. (2008) *A Review of the Evidence on the use of ICT in the Early Years Foundation Stage*, Coventry: British Educational Communications and Technology Agency.

Burgess, S., Hecht, S. and Lonigan, C. (2002) 'Relations of the home literacy environment (HLE) to the development of reading-related abilities: a one-year longitudinal study', *Reading Research Quarterly*, 37(4), 408–426.

Burnett, C. (2010) 'Technology and literacy in early childhood educational settings: a review of research', *Journal of Early Childhood Literacy*, 10(3), 247–270.

Chambers, B., Cheung, A., Slavin, R., Smith, D. and Laurenzano, M. (2010) *Effective Early Childhood Education Programmes: A best-evidence synthesis*, Reading: CfBT Education Trust.

Cordes, C. and Miller, E. (eds.) (2000) *Fool's Gold: A critical look at computers and childhood*, College Park, MD: Alliance for Childhood.

Cordes, C. and Miller, E. (eds.) (2004) *Tech Tonic: Towards a new literacy of technology*, College Park, MD: Alliance for Childhood.

Cox, M., Abbott, C., Webb, M., Blakeley, B., Beauchamp, T. and Rhodes, V. (2003) *A Review of the Research Literature Relating to ICT and Attainment – ICT in Schools Research and Evaluation Series*, 18, Coventry: British Educational Communications and Technology Agency.

Cronin, V., Farrell, D. and Delaney, M. (1999) 'Environmental print and word reading', *Journal of Research in Reading*, 22(3), 271–282.

Cuban, L. (2001) *Oversold and Underused: Computers in the classroom*, Cambridge, MA: Harvard University Press.

de Jong, M. and Bus, A. (2003) 'How well suited are electronic books to supporting literacy?', *Journal of Early Childhood Literacy*, 3(2), 147–164.

Department for Education (DfE) (2012) *Statutory Framework for the Early Years Foundation Stage: Setting the standards for learning, development and care for children from birth to five*, Runcorn: Department for Education.

Everett, D. (2012) *Language: The cultural tool*, London: Profile Books.

Flower, L. (1994) *Construction of Negotiated Meaning: A social cognitive theory of meaning*, Oxford University Press.

Gamble, N. (2000) 'Introduction: new literacies, new technologies?', in Gamble, N. and Easingwood, N. (eds.) *ICT and Literacy: Information and communications technology, media, reading and writing*, London: Continuum, pp. 1–8.

Garrison, M. and Christakis, D. (2005) *A Teacher in the Living Room?*, Menlo Park, CA: Kaiser Family Foundation.

Goodwyn, A. (2000) '"A bringer of new things": an English teacher in the computer age', in Goodwyn, A. (ed.) *English in the Digital Age: Information and communications technology and the teaching of English*, London: Cassell.

Grabe, W. and Kaplan, R. (1996) *Theory and Practice of Writing*, London: Longman.

Grimshaw, S., Dungworth, N., McKnight, C. and Morris, A. (2007) 'Electronic books: children's reading and comprehension', *British Journal of Educational Technology*, 38(4), 583–599.

Healy, J. (1990) *Endangered Minds: Why children don't think and what we can do about it*, New York: Simon & Schuster.

Healy, J. (1998) *Failure to Connect: How computers affect our children's minds and what we can do about it*, New York: Simon & Schuster.

Hallet, E. (1999) 'Signs and symbols: environmental print', in Marsh, J. and Hallet, E. (eds.) *Desirable Literacies*, London: Paul Chapman, pp. 52–67.

Justice, L. (2006) 'Evidence-based practice, response to intervention, and the prevention of reading difficulties', *Language, Speech and Hearing Services in Schools*, 37(4), 284–297.

Justice, L. and Kaderavek, J. (2002) 'Using shared storybook reading to promote emergent literacy', *Teaching Exceptional Children*, 34(4), 8–13.

Justice, L., Skibbe, L., Canning, A. and Lankford, C. (2005) 'Pre-schoolers, print and storybooks: An observational study using eye movement analysis', *Journal of Research in Reading*, 28(3), 229–243.

Kempster, G. (2000) 'Skills for life: New meanings and values for literacy', in Gamble, N. and Easingwood, N. (eds.) *ICT and Literacy: Information and communications technology, media, reading and writing*, London: Continuum, pp. 25–30.

Kim, J. and Anderson, J. (2008) 'Mother–child shared reading with print and digital texts', *Journal of Early Childhood Literacy*, 8(2), 213–245.

Korat, O. and Shamir, A. (2008) 'The educational electronic book as a tool for supporting children's emergent literacy in low versus middle SES groups', *Computers and Education*, 50(1), 110–124.

Lankshear, C. and Knobel, M. (2003) 'New technologies in early childhood literacy research: A review of research', *Journal of Early Childhood Literacy*, 3(1), 59–82.

Lonigan, C., Burgess, S. and Anthony, J. (2000) 'Development of emergent literacy and early reading skills in preschool children: evidence from a latent-variable longitudinal study', *Developmental Psychology*, 36(5), 596–613.

Marsh, J. (2003) 'One-way traffic? Connections between literacy practices at home and in the nursery', *British Educational Research Journal*, 29(3), 369–382.

Marsh, J. (2006) 'Global, local/public, private: young children's engagement in digital literacy practices in the home', in Pahl, K. and Rowsell, J. (eds.) *Travel Notes from the New Literacy Studies: Instances of practice*, Clevedon: Multilingual Matters, pp. 19–38.

Marsh, J. (2007a) *Moving Beyond the Early Learning Goals: Digital literacy in the early years*. Paper presented at annual convention of the International Reading Association, Toronto.

Marsh, J. (2007b) 'New literacies and old pedagogies: recontextualising rules and practices', *International Journal of Inclusive Education*, 11(1), 267–281.

McKenna, M., Reinking, D., Labbo, L. and Watkins, J. (1996) *Using Electronic Storybooks with Beginning Readers*, National Reading Research Center Instructional Resource No. 39, Athens, GA: National Reading Research Center.

McLachlan, C. (2007) 'Emergent literacy', in Makin, L., Diaz, C. and McLachlan, C. (eds.) *Literacies in Childhood: Changing views, challenging practice* (2nd Edition), Marrickville, NSW: Elsevier, pp. 15–30.

McPake, J., Stephen, C., Plowman, L., Sime, D. and Downey, S. (2005) *Already at a Disadvantage? ICT in the home and children's preparation for primary school*, Coventry: British Educational and Communication Technology Agency.

Media and Learning Group (2010) *Joint Media Engagement and Learning*, Menlo Park, CA: SRI International.

Miller, E. and Almon, J. (2006) *Crisis in the Kindergarten: Why children need play in school*, College Park, MD: Alliance for Childhood.

Moody, A., Justice, L. and Cabell, S. (2010) 'Electronic versus traditional storybooks: relative influence on preschool children's engagement and communication', *Journal of Early Childhood Literacy*, 10(2), 294–313.

Myhill, D. and Fisher, R. (2005) *Informing Practice in English*, HMI 2565, London: Ofsted.

Ong, W. (1982) *Orality and Literacy: Technologising the Word*, London: Methuen.

Orellana, M. and Hernández, A. (1999) 'Talking the walk: children reading urban environmental print', *The Reading Teacher*, 52(6), 612–619.

Phillips, L., Norris, S. and Anderson, J. (2008) 'Unlocking the door: is parents' reading to children the key to early literacy development?', *Canadian Psychology*, 49(2), 82–88.

Plowman, L. and Stephen, C. (2003) 'A benign addition? Research on ICT and pre-school children', *Journal of Computer Assisted Learning*, 19(2), 149–164.

Plowman, L., McPake, J. and Stephen, C. (2008) 'Just picking it up? Young children learning with technology at home', *Cambridge Journal of Education*, 38(3), 303–319.

Reynolds, D., Treharne, D. and Tripp, H. (2003) 'ICT – the hopes and the reality', *British Journal of Educational Technology*, 34(2), 151–167.

Richards, I. (1924) *Principles of Literary Criticism*, London: Routledge and Kegan Paul.

Rideout, V., Vandewater, E. and Wartella, E. (2003) *Zero to Six: Electronic media in the lives of infants, toddlers and pre-schoolers*, Menlo Park, CA: Kaiser Family Foundation.

Riley, J. (1998) 'Curiosity and communication: language and literacy in the early years', in Siraj-Blatchford, I. (ed.) *A Curriculum Development Handbook for Early Childhood Educators*, Stoke-on-Trent: Trentham, pp. 45–60.

Robinson, R. (1942) 'Plato's consciousness of fallacy', *Mind*, 51(202), 97–114.

Roulstone, S., Law, J., Rush, R., Clegg, J. and Peters, T. (2011) *The Role of Language in Children's Early Educational Outcomes – Research Brief DFE-RB134*, London: Department for Education.

Segal-Drori, O., Korat, O., Shamir, A. and Klein, P. S. (2010) 'Reading e-books and printed books with and without adult instruction: effects on emergent reading', *Reading and Writing*, 23(8), 913–930.

Sénéchal, M. (2006) 'Testing the home literacy model: parent involvement in kindergarten is differentially related to Grade 4 reading comprehension, fluency, spelling, and reading for pleasure', *Scientific Studies of Reading*, 10(1), 59–87.

Sénéchal, M. and LeFevre, J.-A. (2002) 'Parental involvement in the development of children's reading skill: a five-year longitudinal study', *Child Development*, 73(2), 445–460.

Standards and Testing Agency (STA) (2012) *Assessment and Reporting Arrangements: Year 1 phonics screening check*, STA/11/5688, Coventry: Standards and Testing Agency.

Trushell, J. (1998a) 'Juliet makes her mark', *Reading*, 32(1), 29–32.

Trushell, J. (1998b) 'Emergent writer as emergent "reader": Juliet makes her mark II', *Reading*, 32(3), 41–46.

Trushell, J. and Maitland, A. (2005) 'Primary pupils' recall of interactive storybooks on CD-ROM: inconsiderate interactive features and forgetting', *British Journal of Educational Technology*, 36(2), 57–66.

Trushell, J., Burrell, C. and Maitland, A. (2001) 'Year 5 pupils reading an "interactive book" on CD-ROM: losing the plot?', *British Journal of Educational Technology*, 32(4), 389–401.

Turbill, J. (2001) 'A researcher goes to school: using technology in the kindergarten literacy curriculum', *Journal of Early Childhood Literacy*, 1(3), 255–279.

Verhallen, M., Bus, A. and de Jong, M. (2006) 'The promise of multimedia stories for kindergarten children at risk', *Journal of Educational Psychology*, 98(2), 410–419.

Wartella, E. and Jennings, N. (2000) 'Children and computers: new technology – old concerns', *The Future of Children*, 10(2), 31–43.

Wartella, E., Caplovitz, A. and Lee, J. (2004) 'From Baby Einstein to Leapfrog, from Doom to the Sims, from instant messaging to Internet chat rooms: public interest in the role of interactive media in children's lives', *Social Policy Report*, 18(4), 1–19.

Webb, M. and Cox, M. (2004) 'A review of pedagogy related to information and communications technology', *Technology, Pedagogy and Education*, 13(3), 235–286.

Weigel, D., Martin, S. and Bennett, K. (2010) 'Pathways to literacy: connections between family assets and preschool children's emergent literacy skills', *Journal of Early Childhood Research*, 8(1), 5–22.

7
The Reggio Emilia approach to early childhood education

Jane Cox

Overview

This chapter explores the early childhood education system for children from zero to six years old in the prosperous Emilia Romagna region in northern Italy. It explores the pedagogical and philosophical thinking behind the region's particular approach to children's early years educational experience. Key aspects in the philosophical underpinning are the image of the child that is held by educators in the early childhood settings, the importance of respectful listening and the importance of relationships among a variety of stakeholders. The chapter draws together these aspects to reveal the child-centred nature of the Reggio Emilia approach to young children's development and learning.

The chapter also provides a focus on the environment, documentation and reflection of the Reggio experience. Issues relating to commodification and transferability of the Reggio approach are explored. The chapter invites critical reflection of the way in which the Reggio approach compares with existing knowledge of early childhood education in England and other societies, as well as the usefulness of such comparison.

▶

Key Themes

- Philosophical and pedagogical underpinning of the Reggio approach.
- Child-centred approach to teaching and learning.
- Commodification and transferability of the Reggio approach.

Introduction

The city of Reggio Emilia, which has a population of approximately 165,000, has achieved worldwide recognition for the high quality of its innovative early childhood education provision. The early years education system in Reggio is organised into *nidi d'infanzia* (infant–toddler centres for children aged three months to three years) and *scuole dell'infanzia* (preschools for children aged 3–6 years), mostly operated by the municipality. The early years settings are, however, the product of a particular social, cultural, political, economic and historical context. Following bomb damage during World War Two and experience of Facism under Benito Mussolini (Prime Minister of Italy 1922–1943), the community of Reggio Emilia made the political choice to provide early childhood centres. Indeed, as Mercilliott Hewett (2001, p. 95) reports, the first school for young children 'was built literally by the hands of parents using proceeds gained from the sale of a war tank, three trucks, and six horses left behind by retreating Germans'. They wanted to provide an experience that enabled young children to think and act for themselves (Dahlberg, cited in Jackson, 2004); this would act as a solution for the Fascist experience, which had shown them that people who conformed and obeyed were dangerous. Subsequent central government policy decisions in Italy have enabled municipalities to continue to develop their own early childhood services. There are no centralised curriculum guidelines for young children. The first municipal-managed preschool in Reggio was opened in 1963, followed by the first infant–toddler centre in 1970.

Loris Malaguzzi is recognised as the founding father of the Reggio approach, as the 'architect of the pedagogical and philosophical thinking that permeates the Reggio experience' (Rinaldi, 2005, p. 27). Malaguzzi arrived in Reggio in 1946, became the first director of the early childhood centres, and remained there until his death in 1994. Carla Rinaldi, President of Reggio Children (a mixed public–private company), who worked alongside Malaguzzi from 1979 to 1994, describes him as being 'one of the greatest pedagogical thinkers and practitioners of the 20th century' (Rinaldi, 2005, p. 28). However, rather than being named after Malaguzzi, the person (as with the Steiner approach, or the Montessori approach), the particular approach to early childhood education that evolved in this area of Italy has been named after the place, Reggio Emila. This emphasises the close links the approach has with the local community. Indeed, the Reggio Emilia approach can be described as a collaborative, local 'cultural project on childhood' (Dahlberg and Moss, 2005, p. 180). It takes a localised, communal, child-centred approach to teaching and learning rather than following a prescribed national curriculum.

The Reggio approach has been influenced by a number of key theorists, including Vygotsky, Dewey, Froebel, Bronfenbrenner and Piaget (see Mercilliott Hewett, 2001, and Soler and Miller, 2003, for some useful discussion). Moss and Petrie (2002) use the early childhood centres in Reggio as an example of the many possibilities of 'children's spaces', which for adults and children 'are places where meanings are kept open, where there is space for critical thinking, wonder and amazement, curiosity and fun, learning by adults as well as children, where questions may be asked to which answers are not known' (p. 110). The concept of 'children's spaces' stands in contrast to the instrumental and controlling approach of 'children's services' (evident in England), which Moss and Petrie, writing in 2002, state 'links institutions for children in their many forms to narrow policy agendas (e.g. learning goals, readiness for school, childcare) and their concern to find ever more effective technologies for governing children' (p. 110). Examining the Reggio approach thus enables us to think differently about young children.

The remainder of this chapter seeks to provide some insight into the philosophical and pedagogical thinking that permeates the Reggio approach as well as considering issues of commodification and transferability. Key points will be summarised and questions provided to help provoke further discussion and reflection.

The image of the child: the rich child

Rinaldi (cited in Moss and Petrie, 2002, p. 22) states: 'When we choose the image of the child, we make a pedagogical and political choice. Who is the child? What image do we have?' Asking questions about the image of the child, as they do in Reggio, demonstrates an awareness that different images of the child are possible: 'highlighting what the child *is, can be* and *can* do, or on the contrary emphasising what the child is *not* and does *not have*, what he or she *cannot be* or do' (Rinaldi, cited in Dahlberg and Moss, 2005, p. 136). The image that is chosen will have consequences for policy, provision and practice.

In the Reggio early childhood settings, the 'image of the child is rich in potential, strong, powerful, competent' (Malaguzzi, cited in Moss *et al.*, 2000, p. 250). The children in Reggio are viewed as capable learners, as protagonists in their learning, with the ability to question and to actively participate in the co-construction of knowledge and culture. The children are perceived as being born with a desire to learn, with a wealth of talent and the ability to succeed. The image of the child in Reggio is summed up beautifully by Malaguzzi (2004) when he speaks of children being given the freedom to 'move and shake the world'. Reggio children are viewed as curious, creative beings with multiple ways of expressing themselves; they have a 'hundred languages' and a hundred more. Such expression can take the form of, for example, drawing, painting, drama, puppetry, music, sculpture, words, model-making, photography, tape-recording, shadow play and movement. The image of the child as active, as 'rich in potential, strong, powerful, competent', rejects an image of the child as passive, as 'weak, poor and needy' (Moss and Petrie, 2002); children are therefore seen positively and as having rights to a 'rich' learning experience rather than being viewed negatively and as simply being 'in need'. That all children are viewed as having 'special rights' highlights the inclusive ethos of the Reggio approach (Jennings, 2005). For Mercilliott Hewett (2001, p. 96), 'The critical belief that the child possesses rights is the foundation on which the Reggio Emilia approach is built.'

The image of the child in Reggio has consequences for how others, notably teachers and parents, are constructed. The image of the child as 'rich, strong, powerful and competent' leads on to an image of teachers and parents as also being 'rich, strong, powerful and competent' and, like the children, as having the capacity for further development. The image that is held of the child in Reggio also has important implications for practice and influences the way that the children's learning experiences are constructed, delivered and interpreted in the settings.

Pedagogy of listening

Reggio's image of the child as 'rich in potential, strong, powerful, competent' has consequences for those working with them. As children are viewed as legitimate rights holders with entitlements to a rich learning experience, they are, in their entirety, taken seriously and respected. The 'hundred languages' of children places responsibility on teachers to listen to children's multiple forms of expressing themselves. The 'pedagogy of listening' recognises not only that children express themselves in a variety of ways but also that different children express themselves in different ways and that the environment affects (positively or negatively) children's capacity for expressing themselves (Jennings, 2005, p. 90). Rinaldi (cited in Moss *et al.*, 2005, p. 4) argues that listening only to dominant languages, particularly the verbal and the written, supports 'the power, not only of certain knowledges, but also of certain classes'. Focusing only on particular 'languages' denies children opportunities for expressing themselves. Listening to the multi-sensory 'hundred languages' is thus respectful listening as it involves 'being open to the Other, recognising the Other as different and trying to listen to the Other from his or her own position and experience and not treating the Other as the same' (Dahlberg and Moss, 2005, p. 100).

In the Reggio approach teachers work cooperatively in pairs with groups of children, with the teacher–child ratio varying according to the age group of the children. The teachers undertake the important task of observing and listening to the multiple languages of children. Such a task is not easy since, as Moss *et al.* (2005) point out, many of the 'hundred languages' of childhood have been lost by adulthood. Teachers therefore have to 'tune in' to children. They listen with all their senses and, in doing so, can then use this listening to co-construct children's learning experience rather than just being a transmitter of knowledge. The teachers avoid making assumptions about children, are open to the unexpected, are prepared to be surprised, and respond appropriately by introducing new possibilities into their pedagogical practice in order to enrich the children's learning experience. Thus in the Reggio approach there is a strong commitment to developing 'deep, deep insight of children by listening to them' (Nutbrown and Abbott, cited in Waller, 2009, p. 76). Time is given for teachers to reflect on, interpret and discuss what they have learned from listening to the many languages of children. The 'pedagogy of listening' underpins the image of children that is held in the Reggio approach: 'If we believe that children possess their own theories, interpretations and questions, and are protagonists in the knowledge-building processes, then the most important verbs in educational practice are no longer "to talk", "to explain" or "to transmit" . . . but "to listen"' (Rinaldi, cited in Dahlberg and Moss, 2005, p. 97).

The 'pedagogy of listening' also applies directly to the children. Children are born with a predisposition to listen and quickly notice that listening is required for communication (Rinaldi, 2005). In Reggio, children are encouraged to listen to others (adults and children) as well as to themselves, thus promoting self-learning.

Pedagogy of relationships

While the image of the child in Reggio is 'rich in potential, strong, competent and powerful', it is also 'most of all, connected to adults and to other children' (Malaguzzi, cited in Moss *et al.*, 2000, p. 250). This highlights the importance attached to relationships in the early years education system in Reggio. Indeed, Brooker (2005, p. 128) argues: 'The most important reminder from Reggio for other early childhood settings may be the emphasis on *relationships* as the foundation for children's development and learning.' Citing the work of Sylva *et al.* (1976) she further comments: 'Too much of western pre-school education has been based upon solitary explorer models derived from developmental psychology' (Brooker, 2005, p. 128). In Reggio, children are not viewed as isolated individuals in their learning but as always in relationships with others – teachers, other children, parents and others in the wider community. 'Children *are* seen as individuals, but what matters most is their place within the community of the preschool and its neighbourhood' (Anning, 2009, p. 70). Children, parents, teachers and members of the wider community all participate in the learning process on an equal footing, thus highlighting the egalitarian nature of the Reggio approach. It is a collaborative partnership that is highly valued and 'children learn that collaboration is a powerful experience' (Rogers, 2007, p. 137). Such collaboration is multi-dimensional; it includes relationships between children and teachers, children and children, children and parents, children and other adults, teachers and other colleagues, teachers and parents. There is no hierarchical relationship among the teachers in the Reggio settings.

Children stay together in the same groups with the same teachers during their time in the *nidi d'infanzia* and then in the *scuole dell'infanzia,* thus ensuring continuity and facilitating the development of trusting relationships. Children and teachers work as partners in the learning process – it is a reciprocal process of co-constructing the learning experience, one that enables children to think and act for themselves. A lot of emphasis is placed on the role of parents in supporting the children's development and learning. Reggio early childhood education settings are also linked to the wider community with, for example, carpenters, water workers, musicians and actors being involved in the children's learning experience. Links with the wider community are also evident by the way in which the children's work is proudly displayed in civic buildings in the city of Reggio Emilia. The pedagogy of relationships reflects an important aspect of the social and cultural values that underpin the Reggio approach in which everyone feels 'a sense of belonging' and 'part of a larger endeavour' (Llewelyn Jones, 2004, p. 128, citing the work of Rinaldi, 1998).

Child-centred learning

Dahlberg and Moss (2005) suggest that presenting Reggio as a curriculum model, as many do, fails to recognise a key aspect of Reggio's otherness; terms related to the concept of a curriculum, such as 'curriculum planning', do not provide an appropriate match for the way learning is constructed in Reggio. In Reggio there is no prescribed, written curriculum; learning 'does not proceed in a linear way, determined and deterministic, by progressive and predictable stages' (Rinaldi, cited in Moss and Dahlberg, 2005, p. 106). Instead, learning is based on developmental principles, which place children's interests and needs at the heart of the learning process. Malaguzzi (cited in Mercilliott Hewett, 2001) states that Reggio children are 'authors of their own learning'; the learning experience starts from the child and Reggio children then embark on a voyage of discovery in which they make decisions about their learning. Children initiate, develop and refine their ideas about what they wish to learn and the role of the teacher is to use their knowledge of child development to facilitate, guide and encourage the learning process. Learning is thus very much child-led, with the adult 'teaching to the rhythm of the child' (Sharkey, 2004, p. 157). Such an approach recognises that all children are not the same and therefore require a learning experience that responds to individual differences.

While certain general learning outcomes might be desired in Reggio, the point is that space is left for the unexpected, for new possibilities – the adult does not know where the journey will end and therefore it is not possible to predict what the children will learn. It is a complex process, one in which the adults are also learning, and is therefore a collective voyage of discovery. This complex and dynamic process is captured by the way in which the learning experience in Reggio is likened to a game of ping pong, in which the teacher sometimes catches the ball that the child throws to them, sometimes misses the ball, but if they do not return it the game is finished (Clark, 2005, p. 129). Thus the teacher needs 'an ability to take stock of a situation, to know when to move and when to stay still' (Rinaldi, 2005, p. 27) in order to maximise children's development and learning. Through the information they provide about their child, parents make a valued contribution to the child-centred approach in Reggio; without this information the teachers would be unable to 'teach to the rhythm of the child' (Sharkey, 2004).

Learning takes place in small groups through project work, a dynamic process in which learning takes many different directions and which enables different subject areas to be integrated. The children are encouraged to fully develop their thoughts and ideas in order to explore the chosen topic in depth through play.

Time is thus an important concept within this child-centred approach – children are given time to develop a project and 'the time allowed is notably as long as necessary for the task in hand; a project might last a day, a week or a year' (Fawcett, 2000, p. 119). Children use a variety of modes of expression from the many available in the 'hundred languages'. This contributes to children's learning since, as Forman (cited in Mercilliott Hewett, 2001, p. 99) explains, it enables them to 'confront new possibilities and generate new questions that would not have occurred had they only used one medium'.

Creativity has always taken a central place in the Reggio experience and each setting employs a practising qualified artist – the *atelierista,* with their own studio space, the *atelier* – to work alongside the children on their projects. Projects often involve links with the wider community, such as the making of a table that involved the collaborative efforts of children and local carpenters. In another project an initial idea about creating a lake for birds developed into an amusement park for birds, with the local water workers coming in to help build a fountain. Each project is documented using a variety of methods.

The environment

The environment plays an important role in determining quality in any early childhood education setting and 'is more than simply the planned space in the setting, it is everything that is encountered from point of entry to the setting to point of departure. It also includes the resources in the setting; the images that are promoted; and the messages that these convey what the setting is about' (Langston and Abbott, 2005, pp. 70–71). With regard to the Reggio settings, Malaguzzi stated: 'We place enormous value on the role of the environment as a motivating and animating force in creating space for relations, options, and emotional and cognitive situations that produce a sense of well-being and security' (in Rogers, 2007, p. 137). The provision of a rich environment is thus seen to make an important contribution to the children's learning experience and general wellbeing and is modified by children and staff accordingly in order to respond to the changing needs and interests of the children. Reggio children are seen as having 'a *right* to a rich, complex environment – one that provides a wealth of sensory experiences' (Thornton and Brunton, 2005, p. 33, my emphasis). Such is the importance attached to the environment in Reggio that it has been described as the 'third educator' (Edwards *et al.*, cited in Langston and Abbott, 2005, p. 71).

The fixed structures are a key part of the environment and much attention is therefore given to the architectural design of the buildings. Consideration has been given to the child's-eye view, and glass and light are used effectively to bring the outdoor environment indoors to stimulate children's learning. Lesley Abbott (in Rogers, 2007, p. 137), after visiting the Reggio settings, describes how:

> distinctive in all the . . . preschools is the piazza: the central meeting place where children from all around the school share their play and conversations together. The tetrahedron with the mirrored interior is often to be found there, with children sitting or standing inside it with their friends, looking at themselves, and many versions of themselves . . . mirrors proliferate in all the centres in keeping with the central philosophy of 'seeing oneself' and of constructing one's identity.

Children's work is openly displayed in the classrooms; this is part of the documentation process (discussed below) serving as an inspiration for children, teachers and hopefully also parents and the wider community in the development of further possibilities for children's learning.

Documentation and reflection

Pedagogical documentation can be used to form judgements about children's progress in meeting developmental norms. Dahlberg and Moss (2005) warn that, if used in this way, documentation 'can be viewed as a potential act of power and control, just another device for better governing the child' (p. 108). In Reggio, however, documentation is used to resist power. Collaborative critical reflection on the pedagogical documentation, by adults and children, provides the means for exposing different interpretations, making it possible to challenge what is taken as given about the child. In this way 'they have been able to transgress the idea of a lacking and needy child' (Dahlberg and Moss, 2005, p. 109) that is evident in developmental psychology theory. This process of documenting children's learning, along with shared reflection and discussion, 'supports the ideological concept of the transparent school' (Waller, 2009, p. 77). In this way, as Soler and Miller (2003) point out, documentation provides a response to the criticism that the absence of a written curriculum in the Reggio approach means there is a lack of accountability to the wider society.

Various methods are used to document children's learning during their project work, such as written observations, photographs and video material of a project as it develops, and children's artwork. This provides the basis for continuous reflection on the learning that has taken place and for making decisions as to what needs to follow, and not for intervening in, and controlling, children's learning. Documentation is thus an important assessment tool, but, as Chilvers

(2005, p. 171) argues, it 'respects the way in which children learn and the processes they are involved in, rather than a statistical product'.

Such documentation is also an important part of the respectful 'pedagogy of listening' by ensuring that what Rinaldi (cited in Rogers, 2007) describes as 'visible listening' takes place. Since the process of documentation in Reggio is an open one, it is available for anyone who wishes to participate in reflecting on the children's development and learning – children, teachers, parents and members of the wider community. This can lead to multiple interpretations of the same event; the different questions and possibilities this raises can then be used effectively to promote children's further development and learning.

Mercilliott Hewett (2001) discusses the role of the Reggio teacher as a researcher and the place of documentation and reflection within this. The teacher observes and listens to the children, following up with the collection and analysis (reflection) of data (the documentation). Through this analysis the teacher is able to generate deeper knowledge and understanding about children's development and learning, which can then be used purposefully to help plan the next step in the learning experience.

Commodification and transferability

Reggio Emilia has achieved international acclaim for its approach to early childhood education. Its popularity and influence has been aided by the study tours that have been organised, which permit early childhood educators to observe, and study, the Reggio approach. In addition to the study tours, an exhibition of the Reggio approach, which has toured the world since 1981, has enabled it to reach a wider audience. Together, the study tours and exhibition have been a source of inspiration for early years academics and practitioners alike, and they, along with publications, are part of the accountability to the wider society. The early childhood settings in Reggio are also linked to those in various countries, such as Italy, Australia, the United States, Korea, Japan, the United Kingdom, Germany, the Netherlands, Sweden, Norway, Denmark, Finland, Iceland, Brazil and Peru. The Reggio approach has seemingly become a commodity, a product that has been packaged and exported to a number of countries.

The commodification of the early childhood education system in Reggio has led to concerns among some authors. Johnson (1999, p. 63), for example, expresses his astonishment at the 'fanaticism with which Reggio is engulfing early childhood education'. He draws upon Foucault's work on power relations to raise concerns about the way in which the Reggio approach has attracted our collective psyche. Johnson likens the large-scale adoption of the Reggio approach in the United States to the adoption of 'a type of cargo cult mentality, as we ("locals") too are so "impressed" that we seemingly unequivocally trust Reggio Emilia with what amounts to very little intellectual debate' (Johnson, 1999, p. 68). He claims that the way in which the Reggio approach has tended to be uncritically imported and supported as a cargo cult, as perhaps 'one of the best preschool education systems in the world' (Edwards *et al.*, cited in Johnson, 1999, p. 64), is similar to Foucault's 'regimes of truth'. Johnson goes as far as to question whether the Reggio approach really exists. He argues: 'Reggio does not bring any new or reconceptualized theory to the table. Much of what Reggio offers . . . are the cornerstone features upon which early childhood education programs . . . around the world have been built' (Johnson, 1999, p. 71). Is the Reggio approach really innovative, or is it that we have just pretended that it is a fancy new model that we must own (Johnson, 1999)?

Leaving aside Johnson's concerns outlined above, it is highly questionable as to whether it is possible to transfer or replicate an early childhood education system for, as Moss and Petrie (2002, p. 148) state:

> each policy or provision is the product of a unique context. The uniqueness of that context is woven from numerous threads, coloured by a particular time, place and history: the social actors, both children and adults; the social, political, cultural and economic conditions; the understandings, discourses and values; and the political and ethical choices made in answer to particular questions.

This uniqueness is confirmed by Rinaldi (cited in Moss and Petrie, 2002, p. 148) in relation to the Reggio approach: 'We do not offer a recipe, nor a method, our work is not be copied because values can only be lived not copied.'

However, looking at examples of education systems in different countries can help us to think critically about provision in our own country. Dahlberg and Moss (2005) refer to this as border crossing, arguing that 'we need the provocation of different perspectives' (p. 23). Such provocation can help us to reflect on what we have, to question our own practice, to challenge what we take for granted and to consider what might be possible. This critical thinking can be used purposefully to help improve provision for young children.

An example of Reggio's influence in England has been the development of the Mosaic approach (Clark and Moss, 2001) – a flexible, multi-method approach for researchers and practitioners to listen to young children's perspectives on their experience within their early childhood setting. Although the approach to early childhood education in Reggio is unique to the context (social, political, cultural and economic) of that particular region in Italy, it is possible to adopt elements in relation to one's own culture and resources. The Reggio approach has, undoubtedly, been a key source of inspiration for early childhood educators and academics across the globe. Its 'capacity to provoke is perhaps one of the greatest and lasting legacies of any personal encounter with the Reggio Emilia experience' (Nutbrown and Abbott, cited in Waller, 2009, p. 77).

Conclusion

The Reggio Emilia approach to early childhood education evolved from the vision of Loris Malaguzzi and the commitment and involvement of parents. It has been influenced by the work of many theorists and has achieved worldwide acclaim for the high-quality learning experience it offers young children aged zero to six years. Some key features of the Reggio approach are the image of the child as 'rich in potential, strong, powerful, competent'; a respect for children as rights holders; a focus on listening to the 'hundred languages' of children; an emphasis on collaborative, egalitarian relationships; a child-centred approach to teaching and learning; creative project work; a rich environment; documentation of children's learning; and reflection on children's learning.

The absence of a planned curriculum means that children, and teachers, embark on a 'voyage of discovery' – the endpoint of children's learning is unknown at the outset. This is especially important since, as Rinaldi (cited in Mercilliott Hewett, 2001, p. 98) has poignantly highlighted, 'the potential of children is stunted when the endpoint of their learning is formulated in advance'. However, the Reggio approach is not without its critics. Johnson (1999) expresses concern about the way it 'has been *thrust* upon the field of early childhood education' (p. 63), arguing that individual teachers and settings have taken its alleged newness for granted and have been uncritically importing large-scale elements of it into their practice. Johnson does appear to be a relatively lone voice and the majority view is encapsulated in Gardener's comment (in Waller, 2009, p. 77) that the early childhood centres in Reggio Emilia 'stand as a shining testament to human possibilities'.

Reflective Questions

1. In Reggio, the child is constructed as 'rich in potential, strong, powerful, competent'. What implications does this have for practice?

2. In Italy, central government policy has facilitated the development of 'local cultural projects of childhood' and the preschools in Reggio are a classic example of this. What are the possible advantages and disadvantages of such a development?

3. Reggio children initiate and co-construct projects with adults. What impact might this have on children's development?

4. How does the Reggio approach compare with early childhood education policy and provision in England?

5. Soler and Miller (2003, p. 65) state: 'A criticism of the Reggio Emilia curriculum has been that in the absence of a written curriculum there is a lack of accountability to the wider society.' To what extent is a written curriculum necessary in order to ensure such accountability?

6. What are the possible difficulties associated in trying to transfer the Reggio approach to early childhood settings in England?

References

Anning, A. (2009) 'The co-construction of an early childhood curriculum', in Anning, A., Cullen, J. and Fleer, M. (eds.) *Early Childhood Education: Society and culture* (2nd Edition), London: Sage, pp. 67–79.

Brooker, L. (2005) 'Learning to be a child. Cultural diversity and early years ideology', in Yelland, N. (ed.) *Critical Issues in Early Childhood Education*, Maidenhead: Open University Press, pp. 115–130.

Chilvers, D. (2005) 'Re-thinking reflective practice in the early years', in Hirst, K. and Nutbrown, C. (eds.) *Perspectives on Early Childhood Education*, Stoke on Trent: Trentham Books Ltd, pp. 163–179.

Clark, A. (2005) 'Ways of seeing: using the Mosaic approach to listen to young children's perspectives', in Clark, A., Kjørholt, A. and Moss, P. (eds.) *Beyond Listening: Children's perspectives on early childhood services*, Bristol: The Policy Press, pp. 29–49.

Clark, A. and Moss, P. (2001) *Listening to Young Children: The Mosaic approach*, London: National Children's Bureau.

Dahlberg, G. and Moss, P. (2005) *Ethics and Politics in Early Childhood*, Abingdon: RoutledgeFalmer.

Fawcett, M. (2000) 'Early childhood care and education services in Britain', in Boushell, M., Fawcett, M. and Selwyn, J. (eds.) *Focus on Early Childhood: Principles and realities*, Oxford: Blackwell Science, pp. 108–123.

Jackson, S. (2004) 'Early childhood policy and services', in Maynard, T. and Thomas, N. (eds.) *An Introduction to Early Childhood Studies*, London: Sage, pp. 91–107.

Jennings, J. (2005) 'Inclusion matters', in Abbott, L. and Langston, A. (eds.) *Birth to Three Matters: Supporting the framework of effective practice*, Maidenhead: Open University, pp. 89–104.

Johnson, R. (1999) 'Colonialism and cargo cults in early childhood education: does Reggio Emilia really exist?', *Contemporary Issues in Early Childhood*, 1(1), 61–78.

Langston, A. and Abbott, L. (2005) 'Quality matters', in Abbott, L. and Langston, A. (eds.) *Birth to Three Matters: Supporting the framework of effective practice*, Maidenhead: Open University Press, pp. 68–78.

Llewelyn Jones, B. (2004) 'Early childhood education', in Maynard, T. and Thomas, N. (eds.) *An Introduction to Early Childhood Studies*, London: Sage, pp. 122–134.

Malaguzzi, L. (2004) 'The hundred languages of children.' Leaflet on the 2004 UK exhibition of the Reggio Emilia approach, Newcastle: Sightlines Initiative.

Mercilliott Hewett, V. (2001) 'Examining the Reggio Emilia approach to early childhood education', *Early Childhood Education Journal*, 29(2), 95–100.

Moss, P. and Petrie, P. (2002) *From Children's Services to Children's Spaces: Public policy, children and childhood*, London: RoutledgeFalmer.

Moss, P., Clark, A. and Kjørholt, A. (2005) 'Introduction', in Clark, A., Kjørholt, A. and Moss, P. (eds.) *Beyond Listening: Children's perspectives on early childhood services*, Bristol: The Policy Press, pp. 1–16.

Moss, P., Dillon, J. and Statham, J. (2000) 'The "child in need" and "the rich child": discourses, constructions and practice', *Critical Social Policy*, 20(2), 233–254.

Rinaldi, C. (1998) 'Projected curriculum constructed through documentation – progettazione: an interview with Lella Gandini', in Edwards, C., Gandini, L. and Forman, E. (eds.) *The Hundred Languages of Children: The Reggio Emilia approach* (2nd Edition), Greenwich, CT: Ablex.

Rinaldi, C. (2005) 'Documentation and assessment: what is the relationship?', in Clark, A., Kjørholt, A. and Moss, P. (eds.) *Beyond Listening: Children's perspectives on early childhood services*, Bristol: The Policy Press, pp. 17–28.

Rogers, S. (2007) 'Supporting creativity', in Willan, J., Parker-Rees, R. and Savage, J. (eds.) *Early Childhood Studies* (2nd Edition), Exeter: Learning Matters.

Sharkey, A. (2004) 'International perspectives in early years education and care', in Wyse, D. (ed.) *Childhood Studies: An introduction*, Oxford: Blackwell Publishing, pp. 153–158.

Soler, J. and Miller, L. (2003) 'The struggle for early childhood curricula: a comparison of the English Foundation Stage curriculum, Te Whāriki and Reggio Emilia', *International Journal of Early Years Education*, 11(1), 57–67.

Sylva, K., Bruner, J. and Genova, P. (eds.) *Play*, Harmondsworth: Penguin.

Thornton, L. and Brunton, P. (2005) *Understanding the Reggio Approach*, London: David Fulton.

Waller, T. (2009) 'International perspectives', in Waller, T. (ed.) *An Introduction to Early Childhood* (2nd Edition), London: Sage, pp. 63–79.

8
The Singapore context: A Framework for a Kindergarten Curriculum

Lynn Ang

Overview

On 29 January 2003, a new early years curriculum was introduced in Singapore. The launch of the curriculum, entitled *A Framework for a Kindergarten Curriculum in Singapore* (Ministry of Education, 2003a), was a landmark initiative in the early years sector as it marked the beginnings of a nationally endorsed curriculum for all preschool children and an official benchmark of what a preschool curriculum should entail.

At the heart of this chapter is a critical discussion of the Singapore *Kindergarten Curriculum*, with a focus on the issues and debates that surround the interpretation of the curriculum. With close reference to a research study that was carried out to evaluate the curriculum, this chapter will provide an insight into how the curriculum is developed and shaped. It will offer reflections of preschool teachers' perspectives on implementing the curriculum to promote children's learning, with far-reaching implications on parents, children and practitioners' professional practice.

▶

Key Themes

- The early years curriculum across cultures.
- The early years curriculum in the Singapore context.
- Different sociocultural and policy perspectives in delivering the curriculum.

The Singapore Policy Context

Singapore is a small island nation-state in Southeast Asia, with a population of approximately 4 million. The country was a former British colony and is now part of the Commonwealth since gaining independence in 1963. Singapore is made up of three main cultural groups: Chinese, Malay and Indian. Chinese is the dominant ethnic group, making up more than 80 per cent of the population. In recent years, early childhood has become an important part of public policy. Through the work of two main Ministries, the Ministry of Education (MOE) and the Ministry of Community Development, Youth and Sports (MCYS), the government has put in place cumulative measures to regulate and develop the preschool sector. A key driving force is to raise the quality and accessibility of preschool services for all young children.

The introduction of the *Kindergarten Curriculum* is embedded in a policy drive to regulate the provision of early years services in the country. The policy developments leading up to the curriculum are significant. In March 2000, the Singapore government introduced the *Desired Outcomes* (Ministry of Education, 2000) in what was a preliminary attempt to stipulate a common set of goals for preschool education, with a focus on the social, emotional and moral aspects of children's development. Prior to this, the period between the 1980s and 1990s also saw the genesis of several policy developments in the early childhood sector. In 1988, new legislation was introduced in the form of The Child Care Centres Act and The Child Care Centres Regulations Act, which set out explicit policies and procedures for childcare providers. The Acts were aimed at ensuring the licensing, inspection and overall regulation of child care centres. On 2 October 1995, the Singapore government acceded to the United Nations Convention on the Rights of the Child (UNCRC), following the endorsement of the Convention by the General Assembly of the United Nations in 1990. Under the adoption of the UNCRC, the Singapore government made a commitment to protect the human rights of all children in Singapore by recognising their basic rights to survival and to achieving emotional, physical and mental potential.

The millennium decade marked the start of further policy developments. In 2000, an inter-ministerial task force was formed, comprising representatives from the MOE, the MCYS and preschool practitioners. The work of the team was to develop a common training route for the kindergarten and childcare workforce. As a result, in 2001, a joint ministerial body between the MOE and the MCYS was introduced in the form of the Preschool Qualification Accreditation Committee (PQAC). Jointly steered by both ministries, the committee was set up to oversee the standards and quality of preschool teacher training for both kindergarten and childcare sectors in Singapore. The recommendations put forth by the committee included legislating the minimum qualifications of preschool teachers. The committee mandated that by 1 January 2008, all preschool teachers should hold the minimum of a Certificate in Preschool Teaching (CPT) and from 1 January 2009, all new teachers must have five 'O' level credits, including English Language and a Diploma in Preschool Education in Teaching (DPE-T). From 1 January 2013, all teachers are also expected to achieve a minimum of five 'O' level credits, including a pass in English language and a DPE-T to be employed in kindergartens. In addition, the early years accreditations were accompanied by the introduction of government scholarships and funding to support the training of preschool teachers.

Other policy developments initiated by the Singapore government were targeted directly at supporting lower-income and disadvantaged families. For example, in 2006, government subsidies were made available for lower-income families to help with the cost of preschool education, for example through the Kindergarten Financial Assistance Scheme (KiFAS), which provided a subsidy of up to 90 per cent of the preschool fees. In March 2007, the MOE introduced targeted intervention programmes to enhance the school readiness of preschool children, especially those who were educationally disadvantaged. One such programme was the Focused Language Assistance in Reading (FLAiR) initiative, which provided government-funded intensive one-to-one and small-group language support for preschool children to develop their English language skills and prepare them for primary schooling.

In January 2011, a national quality assessment framework was introduced to monitor the quality of preschool services. The Singapore Preschool Accreditation Framework (SPARK) is a quality assurance framework introduced by the MOE to raise the quality of preschools in Singapore. The assessment is aimed at both kindergartens and childcare centres to enhance their overall provisions, including aspects of teaching, learning, administration and management processes, with recommendations for the short-term and long-term improvements of the service. More recently, in 2012, a new development framework, the Early Years Development Framework (EYDF), was introduced by MCYS to enhance the quality of care for very young children from two months to three years of age (MCYS, 2012a). The rationale behind these government initiatives is to raise the quality of the workforce as well as that of preschool services. It is clear that preschool education has become firmly part of the Singapore government's policy agenda.

Within this policy context, the launch of the *Kindergarten Curriculum* in 2003 was therefore part of a succession of policy reforms to improve the provision of early years education. The *Kindergarten Curriculum* aimed to provide a much-needed coherency in introducing a common framework that catered for all preschool children aged three to six years. The document provided for the first time in Singapore an official statement of what a quality preschool curriculum for children aged three to six years should entail.

The impetus for the proposal of the new curriculum was revealed in a press statement published by the Ministry in 2003. First, the introduction of the new curriculum was to 'give kindergarten education providers a clear direction for developing an educational programme that meets the needs of their children physically, emotionally, socially and cognitively' (Ministry of Education, 2003b). Second, the curriculum was to 'provide a guide to good practices in preschool education' (Ministry of Education, 2003b). The development of the new curriculum and the context in which it was developed therefore raised critical issues in the early childhood sector. It highlighted the issue of raising the standards of teacher training and preschool practices. It also revealed the government's concern with the overall quality of the curriculum and provision of early childhood services in the country. This was especially the case for children from vulnerable families, where the aim of the government was to raise the quality preschool education and thereby provide the greatest leverage for these children to access a quality early years provision and develop a firm foundation in lifelong learning.

The Singapore preschool context

The term 'preschool' in Singapore generally refers to childcare centres and kindergartens. These include a range of settings: religious-based childcare centres, workplace childcare centres, private kindergartens and semi-government-funded kindergartens. Preschools in Singapore generally cater for children aged three to six years, although most childcare centres also provide infant care for children aged two months and above. The compulsory school age for children is seven years, when children enter primary one at the start of the school year in January. Unlike primary schooling, preschool education in Singapore is not compulsory and is provided entirely by the private sector.

Childcare centres and kindergartens differ mainly in their function and hours of provision. Kindergartens cater mainly for children aged three to six years and offer daily sessional educational programmes, ranging from a maximum of 2–4 hours per session. Childcare centres provide full or partial day care, generally from 7am to 7pm during the weekdays and 7am to 2pm on Saturdays. All childcare centres are private or non-public establishments. They are registered under the auspices of the MCYS, but are run commercially for profit by the private sector. Unlike kindergartens, there are no government-funded childcare centres, although government subsidies are available for parents and families who are in need of financial support for childcare costs.

The main reasons for this are twofold. First, the primary remit of the MCYS is to support families and the community, and childcare centres are seen as one such mechanism in their provision of 'care' for working parents and families. Second, the running of childcare centres can be costly. As such, the government has maintained a regulatory and administrative role while outsourcing the provision of care to the private sector. As the Director of the MCYS, Mr Lee Kim Hua, explains, it would be a more cost-effective option instead for the private sector, a non-public organisation, to 'be responsible for the management and operation of services, with the government providing financial support' (UNESCO, 2007). The government's role with regards to childcare centres is thus confined to that of regulating the private childcare market and providing targeted funding to low-income families where necessary. The centres are ultimately responsible for the operation, funding and organisation of their own provision, from the maintenance of resources to the training and professional development of staff. While the MCYS regulates and monitors the overall provision and general physical environment of settings, the centres are effectively owned and managed by private organisations and individuals.

Kindergartens, meanwhile, are largely perceived as 'educational establishments', offering a more education-based preschool service, and therefore operate under the auspices of the MOE in terms of their policies and regulations. However, despite these marked contrasts, in practice the differences between childcare centres and kindergartens are not entirely distinct. It is common for most childcare centres, while registered as such under the auspices of the MCYS, to also provide educational programmes for 4–6 year olds. Conversely, it could also be argued that kindergartens, like childcare centres, provide a similar provision of care for preschool children, albeit for a more specific age group and for shorter hours. The distinction between 'care' and 'education' is therefore arguably ambiguous, and this is especially so in discourse, where 'care' and 'education' are virtually inseparable.

A Framework for a Kindergarten Curriculum in Singapore

As with many countries around the world, where preschool education is provided largely or wholly by the private sector, the provision of early childcare and education services in Singapore is extremely diverse. Childcare centres and kindergartens often vary considerably in terms of their programme content and overall teaching and learning approaches (Retas and Kwan, 2000). Kindergartens, for instance, have the autonomy to stipulate their own goals and philosophies, and are free to determine the curriculum offered to children. The effectiveness of each centre or kindergarten is often dependent on popular impressions, measured arbitrarily by the number of children enrolled, parental expectations and the reputation of each setting. A study conducted by Fan-Eng and Sharpe, for instance, revealed that factors such as 'the centre has a good reputation', 'recommended by someone' and 'other siblings are attending the centre' often influence parents' views of the setting. Perceptions of what entails a 'quality' curriculum are also mixed, depending largely on the setting's curricular emphasis, educational philosophy and general pedagogic beliefs (Fan-Eng and Sharpe, 2000; Wong and Lim, 2002).

Given the diversity of the sector, the conceptualisation of the Singapore preschool curriculum was part of a national drive to provide some degree of standardisation of a curriculum which teachers were able to drawn upon and deliver. The introduction of a national preschool curriculum was also in keeping with a wider movement by governments across the world to enhance the quality of early childhood services in their countries. The New Zealand government, for instance, decided in 1990 that a national early childhood curriculum was to be developed, which eventually led to the introduction of *Te Whariki* in 1996. On the other side of the globe in Britain, the *Curriculum Framework for Children 3 to 5* was introduced in Scotland in 2001, following the English *Curriculum Guidance for the Foundation Stage* for children aged three to five years in 2000.

The international trend among governments to develop national pedagogical frameworks in the preschool sector has also been noted by the Organization for Economic Co-operation and Development (OECD) in the report *Starting Strong – Early Childhood Education and Care* (OECD, 2001). The development of the *Kindergarten Curriculum* was therefore very much aligned with international movements in the early childhood field to raise the standards of preschool curriculum and provision in the settings.

The genesis of the curriculum began in 1999, when a steering committee was formed to work with the Ministry to improve the quality of preschool education (Ministry of Education, 2003b). With representatives from the Ministry, the National Institute of Education, preschool and primary practitioners, the vision of the committee was to improve the quality of preschool education in general and to delineate outcomes for preschool education (Ministry of Education, 2003b). From March 2001 to November 2002, a pilot research study was conducted to evaluate the impact of the new curriculum and its implications on teacher training (Ministry of Education, 2003b). A total of 32 non-profit preschool centres across the country participated. A report on the findings of the pilot study indicated that the new curriculum benefited children from low socio-economic backgrounds by providing them with a more holistic foundation for formal schooling. It revealed that 'pupils from low SES (socio-economic status) and non-English speaking backgrounds benefited more from the new curriculum' (Ministry of Education, 2003b).

The title of the curriculum, '*A Framework for a Kindergarten Curriculum*', implies that the target users are kindergarten settings. An informal discussion with one of the committee members confirms this. The *Framework* was initiated by the committee primarily for the semi-government-funded PAP Community Foundation (PCF) kindergartens in order to improve the provision of preschools over which the Ministry has more jurisdiction. However, as a guidance document, the *Framework* provides a reference for preschool teachers to draw upon and plan their curriculum, and to this extent is also applicable for preschool settings in general.

The *Framework* is structured around six areas of learning: aesthetics and creative expression, environmental awareness, motor skills development, numeracy, self and social awareness, and language and literacy. It is accompanied by a compilation of six booklets, each focusing on a specific area of learning, learning goals, and descriptions of practitioners' roles and responsibilities. Alongside these are two DVDs on 'Nurturing Early Learners' and an additional booklet on 'Putting Principles into Practice', which offers guidance for teachers in planning the curriculum, developing the learning environment and monitoring children's development. An overview of the main features of the curriculum is outlined below.

Desired outcomes of preschool education
- Know what is right and what is wrong
- Be willing to share and take turns with others
- Be able to relate to others
- Be curious and able to explore
- Be able to listen and speak with understanding
- Be comfortable and happy with themselves
- Have developed physical coordination and healthy habits
- Love their families, friends, teachers and school

Principles
Principle 1: Holistic development
Principle 2: Integrated learning
Principle 3: Active learning
Principle 4: Supporting learning
Principle 5: Learning through interactions
Principle 6: Learning through play

Putting principles into practice
Practice 1: Starting from the child
Practice 2: Fostering a positive learning climate
Practice 3: Preparing the learning environment
Practice 4: Planning and structuring learning activities
Practice 5: Setting up resources
Practice 6: Observing children

Areas of learning
Aesthetics and creative expression
Environmental awareness
Motor skills development
Numeracy
Self and social awareness
Language and literacy

First, a list of eight desired learning outcomes provides the overarching aims of preschool education. Second, a set of six principles underpins the goals and outcomes for children. These principles provide a guide to developing an educational programme underpinned by a philosophy of play and active learning.

Third, a further set of six principles provides a framework for developing good practice in the settings.

It is evident that the conceptualisation of the curriculum has taken a very different approach to the traditional subject-based framework of the primary school curriculum. Instead, the principles and areas of learning highlight the main areas of interest of preschool children: exploring and making sense of the environment, skills and understanding for communication through language and literature, active learning, and contributing to self and social awareness. The *Framework* as a whole advocates a holistic approach to children's development and learning.

The booklets covering each area of learning consist of a detailed inventory of outcomes, learning goals, and descriptions of practitioners' roles and responsibilities. The *Framework* emphasises the role of the practitioner in preparing the learning environment and creating 'learning centres' around the classroom (Ministry of Education 2003c, p. 31) by offering a range of suggested activities, such as water play, sand play, blocks, art and craft, and different forms of play media from which children can choose. In the section on language and literacy, for example, practitioners are presented with recommended resources, including a list of fiction and poetry books, and suggested activities for daily practice. It states explicitly the task of the educator in enhancing children's language development, and to cultivate in children a 'positive disposition for language learning' (Ministry of Education, 2003c, p. 4). The learning goals for children range from the broad and generic, such as 'display appropriate reading behaviour', to more specific ones, such as 'discriminate between different letter sounds'. Guided by these goals and principles, the *Framework* therefore has clear aspirations for children and educators. It is centred on a series of tasks, activities and goals in helping children develop their literacy skills, and the role of the educators to help children achieve these goals.

The curriculum is prescriptive in stipulating the types and level of reading and writing skills that children need to develop, and is didactic in its approach to education, emphasising that children 'need to know' and 'children also need to . . .' (Ministry of Education, 2003c, p. 34). Significantly, the *Framework* is also underpinned by the pedagogical philosophy of 'play as a medium for learning' and emphasises the value of play (Ministry of Education, 2003a, p. 14).

Issues and challenges

While the introduction of the Kindergarten Curriculum in Singapore marked a significant milestone in the early childhood sector, it also presented issues and challenges, especially in the context of the country's wider educational landscape.

Singapore is a small country of approximately 5.18 million people (Department of Statistics, 2011). Education in Singapore is a highly competitive and valued enterprise. For an island with no natural resources except for its people, the government recognises that an educated workforce is key to the country's survival. Much emphasis has therefore been placed on education and creating an education system which produces students who are not only academically driven but who possess a 'wide range of talents, abilities, aptitudes and skills' (Gopinathan, 2001). The ideal student, as the scholar Gopinathan asserts, would be 'literate; numerate; IT-enabled; able to collate, synthesise, analyse and apply knowledge to solve problems' (Gopinathan, 2001). This stress on academic and scholastic achievements has brought about what Gopinathan describes as an 'ability driven curriculum', which has influenced the way education across the levels is managed.

Such a competitive and driven education system has inevitably influenced parental expectations of their children's academic achievements, and indeed, parents' attitudes towards what it means to excel in the system. This is evident in their demands for a curriculum that emphasises academic achievements, even at preschool level. Studies have shown that the pressures of the education system in Singapore are such that parents want and expect a formal, teacher-directed education, as they deem it necessary and desirable for their children's learning (Ebbeck and Gokhale, 2004; Tan-Niam and Quah, 2000). It is not unusual for parents in Singapore to prepare their children for the academic rigors of the primary school system and provide them with some form of early education to give them a head start (Ebbeck and Gokhale, 2004; Sharpe, 2000). However, this parental demand for a more academic education provision appears to be at odds with the pedagogical underpinnings of the Kindergarten Curriculum, which advocates a pedagogy that emphasises the value and importance of play and stipulates that the daily schedule of activities for children at preschool age should be flexibly designed and 'starting from the child' (Ministry of Education, 2003a, p. 28).

There is recognition in the Kindergarten Curriculum of the child as an active learner, where learning is best supported through opportunities for play and interaction (Ministry of Education, 2003a, p. 11). Even though the curriculum, to an extent, is prescriptive in its specification of activities and goals, the stress is simultaneously on an informal experience of learning. The principles of the curriculum serve as a reminder that the preschool curriculum is not meant as 'just a preparation for the next stage' (Ministry of Education, 2003a, p. 11). The kindergarten stage is to be regarded as important in itself and 'should not be confused with trying to accelerate learning in the kindergarten years by providing children with a simplified primary school curriculum' (Ministry of Education, 2003a, p. 11). This assertion in the *Framework* about what a preschool curriculum should entail is the clearest indication yet of the complex dichotomy and tension that surround the curriculum: where the pedagogic vision is for a less academic and informal experience of learning but parental and societal pressures are forcing the curriculum into a more formalised model of learning (Ang, 2006).

In 2006, a small-scale study funded by the British Academy was undertaken to investigate teachers' views on the Kindergarten Curriculum. Significantly, the study raised further issues and challenges that underpin the delivery of the curriculum. The main purpose of the study was to explore preschool teachers' perceptions of the curriculum. It aimed to identify the challenges that practitioners face in implementing the *Framework*: the issues, the benefits and the strategies in helping them better understand and implement the new curriculum (Ang, 2006, 2008).

The study was based on a qualitative approach, with the use of face-to-face interviews as the main method of enquiry. A sample of 15 teachers from three preschool settings was recruited, five from each setting. The settings were chosen to reflect the diversity of preschool provision in terms of their location, type and socio-economic stratum of families which they serve. These included a childcare centre and two kindergartens.

Setting one is a privately owned childcare centre located in the Queensway area, in the western part of the island. The setting's fee structure at S$1,312.50 per month for full days and S$829.50 per month for half a day is almost 50 per cent more than the national average cost of childcare at $647 (MCYS, 2012b). The cost marks out the setting's clientele at the higher end of the market.

Setting two is a private, non-profit kindergarten attached to a church. It is located in the housing estate of Serangoon, in the north-eastern part of the island. According to the centre's records, the majority of the families come from the lower to middle income group, with a proportion of the parents having manual or non-professional occupations. The average monthly income for families of children who attend the centre ranges from S$2,000 to S$4,000, with the majority of families falling into the lower end of the spectrum.

Setting three is a partially government-funded, PCF kindergarten, situated in the south of the island, in the housing estate of Woodlands. The setting caters mainly for the average income group of families from the surrounding local neighbourhood.

The findings of the study revealed three major issues:

1. Parental expectations for a more academic approach to the curriculum as opposed to the less formal approach of the *Framework*.
2. Lack of funding and resources for teachers implementing the curriculum.
3. More training and guidance.

The issue of parental expectations and the impact this has on delivering the curriculum is best understood within the country's wider educational context. As discussed in the previous section, a key aspect of Singapore's education system was to prepare children for an ability-driven, knowledge-based economy, and this inevitably influenced parental expectations for their children's academic achievement. Twelve out of the fifteen teachers in the study acknowledged that parental expectations had a significant bearing on the way they delivered the curriculum. This was because, from the teachers' perspectives, the majority of parents expected a more formal and academic approach to the curriculum, as opposed to the informal and play-based approach espoused by the *Framework*. A quote from one of the teachers stated: 'Generally they (parents) want their children to be taught, the alphabet, spelling, very academic. I think generally parents who send their children to kindergartens they expect their children to be able to spell, read and write.'

The responses from the teachers revealed that parental perceptions of what preschool education should entail is a key factor influencing the way the curriculum is delivered. As another teacher said: 'Three-quarters of parents still think play is fun but not useful. Locally and culturally, our people still think play is just for fun. But if you can emphasise the knowledge of play, the thinking skills . . . play can be something . . . We can explain to them.' There is also a sense that collaboration between preschool teachers and parents would be a way of addressing the issue: 'Parents I think . . . need as much insight into play based [approach] as teachers do, because parents don't understand it, trying to encourage and persuade them (parents), that this is education.'

It became clear that a common perception among parents is that their children receiving a formal, academic-based preschool education would mean a higher chance of doing well later at primary school. All teachers in the study felt that parents were often anxious about their children competing in what they perceived to be an increasingly competitive world of school and work. What the study revealed is therefore a mismatch between teachers' and parents' expectations of preschool education. The teachers shared the perceptions that many parents send their children to preschools in the belief that an academic-oriented preschool programme will put their children on the right track to a successful education. As such, there is a disconnect between what some of the teachers see as the aim of preschool education and what some of the parents expect of their children's education, the primary issue being that the kind of learning that the teachers perceive as contributing to a successful preschool experience is not always the same as parents' perceptions.

Second, a key concern underpinning the Singapore Kindergarten Curriculum as revealed through the study is funding and resources. The lack of funding and resources was brought up by five of the teachers as being a challenge to implementing the curriculum. As Natalie said: 'Resources – normally we don't have enough, so whatever we have we just improvising, especially art and craft areas.' When prompted as to why the setting was not able to order more resources, she replied: 'Budget – tight budget.'

Similarly, another teacher, Opal, said: 'Sometimes, we . . . we don't have that much resource, we try to do our best, but we need more resources.'

It is significant that all five teachers who raised the issue of funding and resources came from setting two, which is a private kindergarten catering for largely low-income families. All four teachers felt that in order to implement the Kindergarten Curriculum, they would require more access to materials and equipment, and therefore more funding for resourcing the areas of learning as identified in the curriculum document. When interviewed, the manager of setting two indicated that all equipment and materials were paid for by income from the setting, and while they strove to allocate a larger budget for resources, the centre's limited income meant this was restrictive. As a private kindergarten, the setting is not eligible for government funding and therefore cannot rely on the government's support for resources. As Sharpe (2000) states, private programmes are not subsidised, 'unlike those operated by community groups' or those run by the government. The implication of this is that the only recourse for the kindergarten to acquire additional funds is to increase its fees. However, with the setting catering predominantly for low-income families, any initiative to increase the fees would have a direct impact on enrolment, and therefore on the overall income and viability of the centre. The overarching concern for the teachers and manager was that central government and those endorsing the implementation of the curriculum are not aware of the needs of young children and of the resources necessary to meet these needs.

This issue of funding and resources is also embroiled in a much wider debate over childcare as part of the private/public sector divide, where early years provision is commonly regarded as services and commodities in the private sector for parents to purchase. This market-oriented provision of early years services, as Colley (2006) suggests, 'has come to seem commonplace in a world of privatised services'. The implication of such a system is that childcare is subject to the market forces of demand and supply, with the majority of settings being run as for-profit businesses, offering childcare to working parents with a lowly paid workforce, low levels of qualifications and often less than desirable working conditions.

Among others, Moss and Brannen (2003) and Cohen et al. (2004) have questioned the sustainability of this system and highlighted the damaging consequences of such an economy on the early years workforce, parents and, ultimately, children. As Moss and Brannen (2003) assert, as care continues to become a marketised commodity, it simply means care work 'is transferred from one group of (unpaid) women to another group of (paid) women' and with the overload of care work, there are 'deleterious implications for the care which these paid carers can provide for their own children and families and for themselves'. As the study reveals, similar issues beset setting two with regards to its financial viability on the one hand and aspirations to enhance the curriculum on the other. The problem with the limited resources that the teachers face can be resolved only with more funding, but the setting's income cannot be supplemented by increasing fees as most parents will not be able to afford the cost, and this has an overall impact on the provision and conditions of the setting, not only for staff but also for the children.

A third and final issue concerning the delivery of the Singapore Kindergarten Curriculum is that of professional training and the role of educators in delivering an 'appropriate' early years curriculum. Research has evidenced the important role of preschool educators in providing children with quality care and education. A number of studies have stressed the role of the educator in facilitating children's learning (Anning and Edwards, 2006; Edwards and Knight, 2001; Pugh and Duffy, 2006; Siraj-Blatchford, 1994). Edwards and Knight (2001) stress that the role of the educator is vital in providing an effective early years curriculum, and in making decisions about what the curriculum should entail and how it can be delivered.

All participants in the study identified the complexities of delivering a new play-based curriculum. Professional training and development were deemed essential in ensuring that an appropriate pedagogy is maintained. All the teachers welcomed further training and guidance on the curriculum. They were keen to find out more about possible training sessions and were willing to attend these development sessions if available. One of the teachers suggested that she would like practical sessions, 'more hands-on training', on designing and setting up the suggested areas of learning in the classroom. Another requested more training on 'classroom observation'. This was reinforced by Hayley, who commented: 'I've already had some training, but if new training, I would like more ideas, for the learning centres. I am very happy to attend.' A teacher from the private childcare centre said that rather than training or guidance, she would have preferred to know more about any evaluations that may have been carried out by the Ministry on the curriculum, on 'whether it has been successful or not', and suggested making links with other preschools to find out how they were implementing the curriculum.

Significantly, the study revealed that all the teachers recognised the importance of their professional role in developing and extending the curriculum to promote children's learning. This reinforces extant research which shows that the implementation of any early years curricula demands high-quality practitioners with the appropriate ability, knowledge and understanding of their professional roles and responsibilities (Dahlberg et al., 2002). Delivering and maintaining a quality curriculum for the benefit of the children in all three settings therefore remains an ongoing challenge.

Conclusion

This chapter has provided an insight into the early years curriculum in Singapore. Significantly, the chapter discussed the competing factors that influence the way in which the curriculum is shaped and delivered. The *Framework for a Kindergarten Curriculum* presents a distinct type of learning experience that is supported by both teachers and parents in providing what is deemed a quality and appropriate curriculum. As the study has shown, educators and parents often have differing ideas and philosophies of how best to educate children and what an appropriate curriculum should entail. This raises important issues not only about what the curriculum aims to achieve but how it is achieved at the point of delivery and implementation.

Reflective Questions

1. Think of scenarios in your practice that help to promote children's learning. How do these reflect your own philosophy and beliefs of how children learn?

2. What factors influence the way a curriculum is shaped and delivered?

3. What is distinctive about the Singapore *Framework for a Kindergarten Curriculum?*

4. From your reading of the chapter, what lessons can be learned about the role of culture and sociocultural values in delivering a curriculum?

References

Ang, L. (2006) 'Steering debate and initiating dialogue: a critical analysis of the Singapore pre-school curriculum', in *Contemporary Issues in Early Childhood (CIEC)*, 7(3), 203–212.

Ang, L. (2008) 'Singapore preschool teachers' responses to the introduction of A Framework for a Kindergarten Curriculum in the context of 3 preschool settings', in *Pacific Early Childhood Education Research Journal (PECERAJ)*, 2(1), 55–81.

Anning, A. and Edwards, A. (2006) *Promoting Children's Learning from Birth to Five*, Buckingham: Open University Press.

Cohen, B., Moss, P., Petrie, P. and Wallace, J. (2004) *A New Deal for Children?*, Bristol: The Policy Press.

Colley, H. (2006) 'Learning to labour with feeling: class, gender and emotion in childcare education and training', *Contemporary Issues in Early Childhood*, 7(1).

Dahlberg, G., Moss, P. and Pence, A. (2002) *Beyond Quality in Early Childhood Education and Care*, London: Routledge.

Department of Statistics Singapore (2011) 'Statistics. Key annual indicators'. Available online at: www.mom.gov.sg/workplace-safety-health/resources/Pages/reports-statistics.aspx.

Ebbeck, M. and Gokhale, N. (2004) 'Child-rearing practices in a selected sample of parents with children in childcare in Singapore', *Contemporary Issues in Early Childhood*, 5(2), 194–206.

Edwards, A. and Knight, P. (2001) *Effective Early Years Education*, Buckingham: Open University Press.

Fan-Eng, M. and Sharpe, P. (2000) 'Characteristics of preschool environments and teacher effectiveness in selected child care centres', in Tan-Niam, C. and Quah, M. L. (eds.) *Investing in Our Future: The early years*, Singapore: McGraw-Hill, pp. 66–283.

Gopinathan, S. (2001) 'Globalisation, the state and education policy in Singapore', in Tan, J., Gopinathan, S. and Ho, W. K. (eds.) *Challenges Facing the Singapore Education System Today*, Singapore: Prentice Hall, pp. 3–17.

MCYS (2012a) *The Early Years Development Framework (EYDF)*. Available online at: http://app1.mcys.gov.sg/PressRoom/EarlyYearsDevelopmentFrameworkEYDF. aspx.

MCYS (2012b) 'Statistics on child care services.' Available online at: www.childcarelink. gov.sg/ccls/uploads/Statistics_on_child_care(STENT).pdf.

Ministry of Education (2000) *Desired Outcomes of Preschool Education, Singapore*. Available online at: www.moe.gov.sg/media/press/2003/pr20030120.htm#AnexC.

Ministry of Education (2003a) *A Framework for a Kindergarten Curriculum in Singapore*, Singapore: Tien Wah Press Pte Ltd.

Ministry of Education (2003b) *Launch of Preschool Curriculum Framework*, joint press release by Ministry of Education and National Arts Council. Retrieved 6 January 2006 from www.moe.gov.sg/press/2003/index.htm.

Ministry of Education (2003c) 'Language and literacy development', in *Ministry of Education, A Framework for a Kindergarten Curriculum in Singapore*, Singapore: Tien Wah Press Pte Ltd.

Moss, P. and Brannen, J. (eds.) (2003) *Rethinking Children's Care*, Buckingham: Open University Press.

Organization for Economic Co-operation and Development (OECD) (2001) *Starting Strong – Early Childhood Education and Care*, France: OECD Publications.

Pugh, G. and Duffy, B. (2006) *Contemporary Issues in the Early Years*, London: Sage Publications.

Retas, S. and Kwan, C. (2000) 'Preschool quality and staff characteristics in Singapore', in Tan-Niam, C. and Quah, M. L. (eds.) *Investing in Our Future: The early years*, Singapore: McGraw-Hill, pp. 53–65.

Sharpe, P. (2000) 'Features of pre-school education in Singapore', in Tan-Niam, C. and Quah, M. L. (eds.) *Investing in Our Future: The early years*, Singapore: McGraw-Hill.

Siraj-Blatchford, I. (1994) 'Some practical strategies for collaboration between parents and early years staff', *Multicultural Teaching*, 12(2), 12–17.

Tan-Niam, C. and Quah, M. L. (eds.) (2000) *Investing in Our Future: The early years*, Singapore: McGraw-Hill.

UNESCO Policy Brief on Early Childhood (2007) 'Inter-Ministerial collaboration in early childhood training in Singapore', No. 24. Available online at: http://unesdoc.unesco. org/images/0013/001374/137413e.pdf (accessed 1 May 2006).

Wong, L. and Lim, A. (2002) 'Early childhood education in Singapore', in Chan L. and Mellor, E. (eds.) *International Developments in Early Childhood Services*, New York: Peter Lang.

9
Conclusion: rethinking curriculum

Lynn Ang

The range of chapters showcased in this book reflects the breadth and depth of current thinking in the field. The chapters as a whole expose readers to a multitude of ideas emanating from diverse learning environments nationally and internationally, and urge readers to reflect on what it means to construct their own understanding of how the curriculum can be designed and shaped to support children's learning and development. Through the discussions on the range of curricula and curriculum-related issues from the *Early Years Foundation Stage* to Reggio Emilia and the *Kindergarten Framework* in Singapore, the authors offer thought-provoking ideas related to why, how and in what context children's learning and development can be supported and extended.

At the time of writing this conclusion, there are yet more developments in the early years sector in England. The newly revised Statutory Framework for the Early Years Foundation Stage (EYFS) curriculum has now been introduced and is due to be implemented in September 2012 (Department for Education, 2012). An independent review of early years professional qualifications has also been commissioned and published by the government. The final report of the review, Foundations for Quality (2012), sets out 19 recommendations on how best to strengthen the qualifications and training of the workforce in order to improve the quality of early years services (Nutbrown, 2012). At the core of the report is the affirmation that raising the status and qualifications of the early years workforce is a determining factor in ensuring the highest possible quality of care and education for all children. It would appear from these developments that early years as a field is continuing to gain prominence in the government's policy agenda. More importantly, these developments signal the importance of maintaining an effective care and education environment to support children's development.

Rethinking curriculum: the curriculum as a journey

Children are competent individuals with the ability to acquire many skills and competencies. Our interpretation of the concept of curriculum must therefore start from the assumption that children are powerful agents, who have the capacity to construct their own meanings of the world around them. Above all, we need to recognise that children are capable of developing their own interpretations of the curriculum, and are masters of their own learning. Early years professionals and all those working directly or indirectly with children need to ensure that they are meeting the best interests of the children by providing a curriculum that not only lays the foundation for their learning but is empowering and enabling.

As we have read from the discussions in this book, there are many different approaches to the curriculum and differing ways of supporting children's learning. If, as we now know from research, children's learning and development take place in a collaborative and participatory process, then we need to rethink our notion of what a curriculum means or indeed entails. By rethinking the concept of 'curriculum', the authors in this book have shown that the curriculum is more than just a predetermined, formal document for teaching and learning; it is more than just an educational framework or a set of learning guidelines. Rather, the curriculum is a journey that takes place in a continuous, uneven and sometimes fragmented process, and one that is sustained by ongoing reflection and participation, and influenced by children's own knowledge and competencies.

It is my belief that one of the most effective curricula is one that takes as its starting point the child's life experiences and immediate environment, as it is only then that children will be able to engage in meaningful learning that is both relevant and successful. It is my hope that after working their way through this book, readers will engage in reflection and dialogue about their own understanding of the curriculum, and participate in fruitful learning experiences in their work with and for children.

References

Department for Education (2012) *Statutory Framework for the Early Years Foundation Stage (EYFS)*, Cheshire: Department for Education. Available online at: www.education. gov.uk/publications/eOrderingDownload/EYFS%20Statutory%20Framework% 20March%202012.pdf.

Nutbrown, C. (2012) *Foundations for Quality – The independent review of early education and childcare qualifications*, Cheshire: Department for Education. Available online at: www.education.gov.uk/publications/standard/publicationDetail/Page1/DFE-00068-2012.

Index

(italics indicate a figure in the text)